Tanushree Podder
Illustrated by Pallavi Jain

HARPERCOLLINS
CHILDREN'S BOOKS

First published in 2024 in India by HarperCollins *Children's Books*
An imprint of HarperCollins *Publishers* India
4th Floor, Tower A, Building No. 10, DLF Cyber City,
DLF Phase II, Gurugram, Haryana – 122002
www.harpercollins.co.in

2 4 6 8 10 9 7 5 3 1

Copyright © Tanushree Podder 2024
Illustration © HarperCollins *Publishers* India 2024

P-ISBN: 978-93-6213-839-2
E-ISBN: 978-93-6213-017-4

The views and opinions expressed in this book are the author's own and the facts, verified as of 30 April 2024 to the extent possible, are as reported by the author. The publishers are not in any way liable for the same. While every effort has been made to ensure that the most significant moments in every sportsperson's journey have been covered in the book, owing to limitations, some may have been excluded.

Tanushree Podder asserts the moral right to
be identified as the author of this work.

All rights reserved. No part of this publication may be reproduced, stored in a retrieval system, or transmitted, in any form or by any means, electronic, mechanical, photocopying, recording or otherwise, without the prior permission of the publishers.

Typeset in 11/16.8 Bookman Old Style by Kamal Kishor

Printed and bound at
Nutech Print Services - India

Dedication

To the Indian sports champions, who embody strength, determination and unwavering passion.

To my husband, Ajoy Podder, a former army athlete, who taught me to never give up

Contents

Preface   9

ARCHERY   13
Deepika Kumari   15

ATHLETICS   20
Annu Rani   22
Avinash Sable   29
Eldhose Paul   36
Hima Das   42
Murali Sreeshankar   48
Neeraj Chopra   56
Swapna Barman   62

BADMINTON   68
Lakshya Sen   69
P.V. Sindhu   77

BOXING   83
Lovlina Borgohain   85
Mary Kom   92
Nikhat Zareen   97

CHESS   104
Praggnanandhaa R.   106

CRICKET   113
Jhulan Goswami   115
Mithali Raj   120
Sachin Tendulkar   125
Smriti Mandhana   132

FOOTBALL   139
Bhaichung Bhutia   141
Sunil Chhetri   146

GYMNASTICS — 152
Dipa Karmakar — 153

HOCKEY — 159
P.R. Sreejesh — 160
Rani Rampal — 168

SHOOTING — 175
Abhinav Bindra — 176

WEIGHTLIFTING — 183
Achinta Sheuli — 184
Jeremy Lalrinnunga — 189
Karnam Malleswari — 195
Mirabai Chanu — 200

WRESTLING — 205
Bajrang Punia — 207
Sakshi Malik — 214
Geeta, Babita, Vinesh Phogat — 219

Acknowledgements — *226*

Preface

A few weeks back, I was on a road trip across the Sahyadri range. As I passed the Malshej ghat, I noticed small groups of children jogging on the road. Dressed in running gear, these children were 10–12 years of age. After passing a few groups, I halted and asked why they were running. One of them, a girl of about 12, said, 'I want to play for India and win a medal.'

Another girl wanted to be an athlete and win medals so she could see her name in the newspapers. A teenaged boy, inspired by Neeraj Chopra's Olympic medal, wanted to take up javelin throw. He confessed he had not heard of the sport until Neeraj had made the historic win. Someone wanted to be a boxer, someone a weightlifter, and yet another wanted to be a pole vaulter or a racewalker. They all dreamt of winning medals and becoming famous. The children were mostly from modest backgrounds and lived in villages or small towns. They dreamed of name and fame, success and wealth.

Their enthusiasm was truly heartening. I was very touched by their sincerity and dedication. Some of these children would perhaps represent India in the international arena someday. So moved was I by their dreams and the determination they had to achieve it that I decided to write this book. Through it, I want to ignite in thousands of children the spark to have and to nurture a dream. I wish for them to learn that behind every success lies a story of triumph over struggles and challenges—we often forget the sweat and tears that paved their way to the top.

I want my readers to know that in order to become an athlete, one must put in the hours, pay special attention to consuming a balanced diet, stay consistent in one's exercising routine. One must have access to the facilities required for practising a sport—equipment, gear, trainers. Sadly, most of our villages lack the infrastructure needed to make a good sportsperson. Many of our athletes come from impoverished families and can barely afford a couple of meals a day, so how would they cater to the special diet, equipment or training?

As you turn the pages of this book, you will come across countless stories of athletes who were forced to practise without proper shoes or had to run barefoot because they could not afford the costly running shoes. Starting with Lovlina Borgohain, who won a bronze medal in the Olympic Games—to Jeremy Lalrinnunga, many athletes came from impoverished families. Hima Das, the Dhing Express from a village in Assam, didn't own a pair of running shoes and practised on an uneven, mud-spattered football field, but brought laurels to the nation by winning five successive golds in a year. Dipa Karmakar, a small-town girl, vaulted into history with the 'Vault of Death', which is a dangerous feat. There are just five gymnasts in the world to perform the Produnova Vault. She is one of them. Swapna Barman is a rickshaw puller's daughter, who could not find proper shoes because she has six toes on each foot. She trained despite the discomfort and pain. The girl brought home India's first heptathlon Gold in the Asian Games in 2017. The Phogat sisters dedicatedly practised in a makeshift pit, dug by their father, as the wrestling stadium denied girls the opportunity to train. Deepika Kumari honed her skills by shooting at hanging mangoes with a bamboo bow and arrow that she made herself. Karnam Malleswari's mother crafted homemade weights for her daughter's weightlifting practice. Neeraj bought his first personal javelin only in 2014. Jeremy practised with bamboo sticks and water pipes. Achinta's family was so poor that he and his brother harvested crops and carried loads on their heads. There are countless such examples.

Yet, these sportspersons refused to succumb to their circumstances. They dared to dream and braved the odds to live their dreams. Their self-belief took them places. Their courage placed them on international podiums and rewarded them with medals. 'The more difficult the victory, the greater the happiness in winning,' said Pele, and rightly so.

These sportspersons live and breathe their sport. No love is greater to them, and no hardship is daunting enough. Their intensity is admirable, and their focus is enviable. They continue to push harder to get where they want to be.

In this collection, I chose stories that helped bring out the difficulties in the path of the athletes and how they endured it all to attain resounding success. The stories are not just meant to inspire young readers but also their parents to help their children maximize their potential and encourage them to take up sports.

Archery

1. The history of archery in India dates to the Vedic era when it was practised as a sport as well as a means of hunting. The Mahabharata and Ramayana refer to archery as a skill of warfare that was imparted to the youth at the time.
2. The Olympic Games introduced archery as a sport in 1900.
3. Baron Pierre de Coubertin is commonly referred to as the founder of modern Olympic Games and was responsible for the inclusion of archery in the Olympics.
4. Target archery, the most well-known form of modern archery, involves shooting up to a distance of 70 metres in a standard competition.
5. The world record for the longest precise shot with a traditional bow and arrow stands at 283.47 metres. It was set by Matthew Stutzman, an American archer who was born without arms—he shoots with his legs and feet.
6. In contemporary archery, when an archer splits an arrow that is already embedded on the target with another arrow, he is known to have achieved the Robin Hood shot. It requires excellent skill to

carry out the feat, so it is named after the legendary Robin Hood, who was an excellent archer.

7. Archers wear arm guards on the forearm to protect the arm.
8. The bullseye refers to the circular centre of a target.
9. The arrow puller is a device used to protect the hand and help pull arrows from the target.

Deepika Kumari: The Ace Archer

The Story

Deepika Kumari was born on 13 June 1994 to a very poor family in the Ratu Chatti village, 15 kilometres from Ranchi. Her father, Shivnarayan Mahato, was an auto rickshaw driver, and her mother was a nurse at the Ranchi Medical College. Life was tough as the family could barely afford one meal a day. Hunger drove Deepika to knock down mangoes by throwing stones at them. To everyone's surprise, the girl never missed her aim. Soon, she began using a catapult to aim at the mangoes.

The Journey

Deepika first heard about archery from a cousin, who was training at the Tata Steel Sports Academy in Jamshedpur. The 11-year-old Deepika was fascinated because the centre provided free food and stay for the students. Thus, Deepika brushed up her archery, using a bamboo bow and some arrows to practise her aim. Her goal at that time was to reduce the burden on her family. Young Deepika had not dreamed she would end up winning so many medals.

Deepika's parents did not want her to leave home and join the academy. But her determination and conviction strengthened her resolve, and she was able to convince her parents. That done, Deepika walked into the Tata Steel Sports Academy to seek admission.

Things did not go according to Deepika's plan. The academy refused to accept her at first. Deepika pleaded with the authorities to give her three months to prove herself. Instead, the academy authorities asked her to join the Arjun Archery Academy in Kharsawan, Jharkhand.

It was here at Kharsawan that Deepika began training to be an archer. Soon, she picked up enough skills to prove her mettle by winning a few local competitions. Word of her success reached Dharmendra Tiwari, a coach at the Tata Steel Sports Academy, who was in search of talented youth. The coach took her under his wing at the academy. At the young age of 12, she finally managed a spot in the academy that had initially turned her down.

Recurve is the traditional form of archery, which uses a bow with a simpler design and the absence of a complex pulley system.

The Tata Steel Sports Academy provided Deepika with her first set of professional equipment and a uniform. Not just that, the academy granted her a stipend of 500 rupees per month, which went a long way in supporting her needs.

After she began training at the Tata Sports Complex in Jamshedpur, it was almost like a dream. She had never stayed in a hostel with separate toilets for women.

Despite the facilities, Deepika felt unsure in the first few months at the academy. She was very young and everything was new for her. She didn't even speak the same language as her peers. All this while, she had only practised with a bamboo bow and arrows, and now she would have to get used to the sophisticated archery equipment.

However, Deepika kept her focus on the sport. She underwent rigorous training to learn all about recurve archery and the technicalities of competitive archery. Her hard work paid off when she participated in the 2006 Archery World Cup held in Mexico. However, she could not win a medal. In addition to the opportunities that playing archery brought, Deepika was also overjoyed to sit in a plane for the first time. At 15, she won the gold medal in the women's individual recurve event at the 2009 Cadet World Archery Championships.

At the 2010 Commonwealth Games held in Delhi, she won two gold medals in recurve women's individual and team competitions. Deepika brought home a silver medal from the 2011 Archery World Cup held in Istanbul. She followed it up with another silver in the recurve women's team event at the World Archery Championships held in Turin, Italy, along with Laishram Bombayla Devi and Chekrovolu Swuro.

There was no looking back. With each event, Deepika's tally of medals continued to increase. The country was stunned and overjoyed by the young archer's victories. Deepika had placed India firmly on the world map.

As a result of her achievements, news reporters and television crew thronged her modest mud house in the dusty lanes of Ratu Chatti village. The village, which few people had heard of, became known to the entire world. Having bagged an impressive tally of medals at international archery competitions, Deepika continued to dazzle the world with her prowess.

Although she entered the 2012 London Olympic Games as World Number 1, Deepika was eliminated in the very first round. It was a disheartening performance for her, but she quickly got over the disappointment and focussed her attention on the next event. The

2014 Wroclaw Archery World Cup provided her with fresh hope and she returned with a gold in the team event.

In 2019, she bagged a bronze at the 2019 Asian Championships in the women's and mixed team before the pandemic brought things to a standstill. In 2021, Deepika created history by clinching three gold medals (recurve women, recurve women team and recurve mixed team) at the World Cup Stage 3 in Paris. This catapulted her rank to number one in the 2021 global archery rankings.

The Tokyo Olympics, which had been postponed because of COVID-19, were announced in 2021. Once again, Deepika's name figured in the list of athletes who had qualified for the Olympics. This was the third time for her.

Like every other sportsperson, Deepika aimed for the Olympics. She tried her hand at the 2012 London Olympics, followed by the 2016 Olympics in Rio and the 2020 Tokyo Olympics. But she had to return empty-handed.

> In 2021, Deepika created history by clinching three gold medals (recurve women, recurve women team and recurve mixed team) at the World Cup Stage 3 in Paris.

There is little doubt that Deepika is one of the best archers in the world, and India is proud of her achievements. She was honoured with the Arjuna Award in 2012, the Padma Shri in 2016 and the Young Achievers Award in 2017.

From shooting down mangoes to winning a gold medal in several international events, Deepika Kumari has come a long way. It has taken many struggles and heartbreaks, but she has steadily progressed towards making a name for herself.

Deepika is an inspiration for every Indian, especially for girls.

Athletics

1. The British used postal runners from one village to relay post to the next, carrying letters on a pole with a sharp point.
2. The World Athletics list of sports includes disciplines such as middle/long running; hurdles; road running; jumps—long, high and triple jumps along with pole vaults; throws—shot put, discus, hammer and javelin; combined events—decathlons and heptathlons; race walks, relays, cross country, mountain running, ultra running and trail running.
3. The first steeplechase started in Ireland, with horses and riders racing through the countryside towards a visible church steeple. During the race, the participants had to leap over streams and small barriers. However, it has undergone significant changes since the inaugural steeplechase race in 1752. Today, steeplechase athletes face the challenge of running over 28 hurdles and clearing 7 water jumps in a 3000-metre course.
4. The length of the long jump runway is 40 metres.
5. Heptathlon is a track-and-field combination of 7 events taking place over two days. The women's heptathlon includes 100-metre hurdles, high jump, shot put and 200-metre run on the first day;

and the running long (broad) jump, javelin throw and 800-metre run on the second day. (Fun fact: hepta means seven!)

6. The Ministry of Youth Affairs and Sports in India launched a scheme called the Target Olympic Podium Scheme (TOPS) in September 2014 to promote sports and help outstanding athletes in reaching the Olympic podium.

7. The Olympic Games motto in Latin is 'Citius, Altius, Fortius', while it is 'Faster, Higher, Stronger' in English. However, this was changed in 2021 to recognize the unifying power of sport and the importance of solidarity. The new motto is 'Citius, Altius, Fortius – Communiter' in Latin and 'Faster, Higher, Stronger – Together' in English.

8. Usain Bolt is known as the fastest man on earth.

9. Milkha Singh earned the nickname 'Flying Sikh' due to his impressive speed in running. With five gold medals in international athletic championships, he was awarded the Helms World Trophy in 1959 for his outstanding performance when he won 77 out of his 80 international races. He also won independent India's first Commonwealth gold in 1958.

10. P.T. Usha was called Payyoli Express by her fans.

1st Indian Woman to Win Gold for Javelin in Asian Games 2022

Annu Rani

Athletics

Annu Rani: The Javelin Doyen

The Story

Annu Rani was born on 28 August 1992 in Bahadurpur, a village in Meerut, Uttar Pradesh. She was the youngest of her five siblings. The village is surrounded by lush green sugarcane fields and is inhabited by about 400 families, most of whom are sugarcane farmers. Like most people in the village, Annu belonged to a Jat family of farmers. As a young girl, she watched her brother take up running and fell in love with the sport. At that time, her ambition was to be a long-distance runner like her brother, Upendra Singh. At times, Annu would join her brother and the other boys to play cricket. During one such cricket match while she was fielding, Upendra noticed her throw the ball from the boundary line. So powerful was her throw that Upendra was convinced that she would be perfect for long-distance throws like javelin.

Most girls from the village spent time doing household chores and were married off at an early age, but Annu had no intention of following them to the wedding altar. She had no interest in making rotis or firing up the hearth either. All she wanted to do was to leave the village and achieve something big.

The Journey

While in school, Annu had to take up a sport of her choice, so she chose javelin throw. However, the javelins provided by the school were made from bamboo, and during the practice sessions, Annu would end up damaging several javelins with her strong and long-distance throws. She also broke a flowerpot while throwing a javelin. After a couple of such incidents, the school stopped providing her with javelins for practice.

That didn't stop Annu from practising her throws. An idea struck the determined girl. There was no dearth of sugarcane around the village, and Annu fashioned javelins from sugarcane stalks and practised with them. One day, Upendra saw her practising with sugarcane stalks while he was playing cricket. This visual only added to his belief that she would be good at javelin throw and he began encouraging her. He asked her to hurl sugarcane sticks in the open fields around the village.

By this time, Annu was in love with the sport and wanted to be a javelin thrower. However, she belonged to a conservative family of farmers, and her father was absolutely against the idea of his daughter taking up sport in any form. Annu, however, was determined. She tried to convince him with arguments, and when he didn't relent, she begged and cried. Amarpal Singh, her father, gave in, thinking she would tire of the sport after a while.

That didn't happen. Instead, Annu continued to practise diligently. Since javelins were expensive and she could not afford to buy one, she continued to use sugarcane as a substitute. Later, she made herself a javelin from a long piece of bamboo. At first, Upendra guided her during practice. However, she needed a professional to help her get the technique right. So far, she would just run and lob the javelin with all her strength as far as she could. She could hurl the javelin over 45 metres, which was very good by any standard. Her skill impressed the physical training teacher, who suggested that she take part in district and state-level competitions.

It was a trying time for Annu, as her conservative family refused to allow her to travel alone outside Meerut. But her teacher met her parents and tried to convince them of her bright future in sports. As a result, it was decided that her brother or father would accompany her during practice sessions and competitions.

Annu's determination and hard work paid off as she began to win medals in school and junior-level competitions. It was during one such competition that Kashinath Naik, the 2010 Commonwealth Games bronze medallist-turned-coach, noticed her potential. First, he spoke to Upendra Singh, who was supportive of his sister's efforts. The brother, who had always supported Annu, agreed.

> Kashinath Naik, the Commonwealth Games medallist-turned-coach, noticed Annu Rani's potential at a junior-level competition.

The Athletics Federation of India (AFI) was impressed with Annu's performance and called her to participate in the Asian Junior Championships in Vietnam that were to take place in 2010. She did not have a passport when she went to the preparatory camp. Annu applied for a passport, but it did not come on time, and she missed going to Vietnam for the games. Her family, who were against her going abroad, were relieved.

In the meantime, Annu's father continued to be reluctant about her training. Upendra and Annu tried to convince him about her bright future in sports. Coach Kashinath also joined forces with them. Amarpal Singh realized his daughter was serious about the sport and finally had to give in. Thus, in 2013, Annu began training at the Netaji Subhas National Institute of Sports (NSNIS), Patiala, under coach Kashinath.

At Patiala, Annu practised hard—she would throw the javelin dozens of times daily and lift heavy weights to improve her strength so that she could hurl the 600-gram javelin with ease. The benefits of professional training were soon reflected in Annu's performance. She showed remarkable improvement in her throws. It was then that Kashinath began to encourage Annu by telling her to watch motivational films on athletes. Thus, he sowed in her the dream of winning a medal at the Olympics. In 2014, Annu took part in the National Inter-State Athletics Championship at Lucknow. She won the gold medal and broke the 14-year-old national record with a throw of 58.83 metres. It was the gold medal that earned her the backing of her father, and there was no looking back. With the record-breaking throw, she also qualified for the 2014 Commonwealth Games in Glasgow, Scotland. She finished eighth at Glasgow, but the very next year she returned with a bronze medal at the 2015 Asian Games at Incheon, South Korea, with a throw of 59.53 metres.

Annu's performance at Glasgow and Incheon boosted her morale. She trained hard and improved her performance. In July 2016, she bettered her national record at the 56th National Inter-State Senior Athletics Championships in Hyderabad with a throw of 60.01 metres. With that, she broke four national records and attained the glory of becoming the first Indian woman to cross the 60-metre mark. By this time, she had begun training under coach Baljeet Singh. In 2019, she became the first Indian woman to qualify for the finals of the women's javelin throw event at the World Athletics Championships, Doha. She won the gold medal with a record throw of 62.83 metres at the 2021 National Inter-State Senior Athletics Championship, Patiala. Despite the gold, she had failed to reach the cut-off mark to qualify for the Tokyo Olympics.

In the meantime, the pandemic had put the 2020 Tokyo Olympics on hold. No one knew what the future held for them. Annu remained quarantined at NSNIS and could not meet her family for one year. But she continued to do several physical exercises in a ground near her hostel to maintain her fitness. She read books on Swami Vivekananda and watched inspirational videos of Cristiano Ronaldo and Michael Phelps to maintain a positive frame of mind.

While preparing for the Tokyo Olympics, Annu suffered a foot injury, which hampered her preparation. Yet, she continued with her training. Her family, village and the entire nation pinned their hopes on her. She failed to qualify for the Tokyo Olympics. There was disappointment all around when Annu could not make it to the final round. Her best throw of 54.04 metres was nowhere near her previous records.

> Though disappointed by her failure to qualify for the Tokyo Olympics, Annu did not lose hope and chose to focus on the upcoming Commonwealth Games.

With a never-say-die attitude, Annu tried to forget her debacle in the Tokyo Olympics and focussed on the 2022 Commonwealth Games, which were to be held in Birmingham, England. Although the leg injury still troubled Annu and hampered her last few strides while throwing the javelin, she continued to pin her hopes on the Commonwealth Games.

This time, Annu was determined not to let her country down. Back in her village, her family and friends sighed with disappointment when two of her throws were declared foul and did not count. They watched anxiously as she hurled the javelin to a distance of 60 metres in her fourth throw and finished third. She scripted history on 7 August 2022, when she became the first Indian female javelin thrower to win a bronze medal at the Commonwealth Games.

Annu proved her mettle again at the Asian Games 2022 by winning the gold medal with a throw of 62.92 metres. She became the first Indian woman to win an Asian Games gold in javelin throw. It was a momentous victory that paved the way to the Olympic Games in 2024.

1ST INDIAN to win a GOLD AT CWG FOR STEEPLECHASE

AVINASH Sable

ATHLETICS

Avinash Sable: The Steeplechase Champion

The Story

Avinash Sable was born on 13 September 1994 in a village called Mandwa in the Beed district of Maharashtra. Mandwa is a remote village of farmers, which lies in a drought-prone area, and so, very few villagers are well off. There is little scope for employment and the water crisis makes it impossible to till the land, so many farmers work in brick kilns or move to the city as labourers.

Like most villagers, Avinash's parents Mukund and Vaishali were also struggling and had to take up work in brick kilns to provide for their three children.

Since Mandwa lacked transport facilities, Avinash would walk nearly 6 kilometres every day to reach school, even as a 6-year-old. The little boy preferred to run rather than walk. He ran about 12 kilometres each day, back and forth from school.

Not just school, Avinash would run all the way to the fields and even run errands assigned by his parents on foot. He loved to run, and it didn't exhaust him. But he never thought of pursuing it professionally. His only ambition was to join the Indian Army so he would be able to provide for his family and support his parents.

The Journey

Owing to Avinash's humble background, money was always a problem. There was never enough money and the family had to go through many hardships.

When he was in class 7, Avinash was selected in a talent scout by the state government. He was sent to Aurangabad for training, but the coaches didn't find him promising and he returned to the village. This was a setback for the entire family, who had hoped for a better future.

For a long time, Avinash's life was set in a rut. He ran to school, studied and ran back. In the little time that remained, he worked with his parents. Any hopes of getting out of the rut were shattered after his rejection at Aurangabad.

In 2013, Avinash fulfilled his ambition when he joined the 5 Mahar Regiment of the Indian Army. He was the first one from his village to have a secure job and a fixed salary. He could afford to send money home and his parents would not have to labour in the brick kilns. This gave him a lot of satisfaction.

During his tenure, Avinash was posted first to Siachen and then to Rajasthan, both of which had extreme weather conditions. Right from a freezing – 30 degrees to a blistering 50 degrees, he went through it all. It was in 2015 that Sable learned about the army's athletics programme and was chosen to participate in the cross-country competitions. Though talented, he lacked training. In the meantime, he also suffered an injury, causing him to gain weight. His athletic career came to a grinding halt. Things took a turn when a cross-country race was announced by his regiment. He was keen to take part, but his weight was a hindrance. Determined to do well, he began practising hard and lost 15 kilograms. Leaner and fitter,

Avinash took part in the cross-country race and did very well. It was here that he was noticed by Captain Amrish Kumar, the coach of the army athletics team.

During one of the practice sessions at the training camp, the sharp-eyed Kumar, a gold medalist in the 3000-metre steeplechase at the 1999 South Asian Games held in Kathmandu, noticed the simple manner in which Avinash leaped over hurdles and suggested that Sable take up the 3000-metre steeplechase.

Avinash, who found the steeplechase interesting, agreed to make the switch and began training under Amrish. Soon after, he started training under the Belarusian coach Nikolai Snesarev at the national camp. Nikolai was a tough taskmaster and had many strictures about diet and practice. He allowed his athletes to eat only boiled vegetables and chicken soup with no spices and permitted just two phone calls a week. The practice was rigorous, and no indiscipline was tolerated. Most athletes found it difficult to adjust, and in 2018, Avinash moved back to his previous coach, Amrish.

> Avinash spent some time training under the Belarusian coach Nikolai Snesarev, who was a tough taskmaster and a strict disciplinarian.

The little time that Avinash spent training with Snesarev had taught him many lessons. After Avinash won the silver in Doha, he didn't allow him to leave the camp. He was invited to several felicitation functions. Some were even ready to fly him, but Snesarev did not allow him to go as he didn't want Sable to get distracted from the sport. Later, Avinash dedicated his success to the tough lessons taught by Snesarev, who died before witnessing his success at the Commonwealth Games. The Belarusian's strict discipline had benefitted Sable immensely.

In 2018, Avinash took part in the Indian Open Championship at Bhubaneswar and broke the 30-year national record by clocking in 8:29.88 in the 3000-metre steeplechase. This was a vindication of his coach's belief and hard work.

In 2019, he clocked 8:28.94 in the Federation Cup in Patiala, breaking his own national record from 2018. From a long-distance runner, Avinash became a champion steeplechaser. 2019 proved to be a golden year as he broke the national record three times.

In 2019, Avinash made his debut in international athletics in Doha. He finished 13th in the 2019 World Championships held in Doha. This disheartened him, but athletics is never predictable. An athlete doesn't win a medal at every event, nor did Avinash.

The tide soon turned and he won a silver medal at the 2019 Asian Championships in Doha. The medal motivated him.

However, Sable wasn't satisfied. He had been eagerly awaiting the qualifying race for the 2020 Tokyo Olympics in the 3000-metre steeplechase. He ran three seconds faster than his national record time but failed to qualify. It was only when the AFI appealed against his obstruction by another runner that he was allowed to enter the last stage. Thus, he qualified with a time of 8:21.37 and became the first Indian to qualify for the Olympics steeplechase event since Gulzara Singh Mann in 1952.

Unfortunately, the 2020 Tokyo Olympics were postponed due to COVID-19 and a dejected Avinash went back to his village. In the meantime, the Maharashtra government announced an assistance of 50 lakh rupees to help him prepare for the Tokyo Olympics.

In November 2020, he took part in the Delhi Half Marathon, just to test himself. This time, he clocked 1:00.30 and became the first Indian to run a half marathon in less than 61 minutes. The previous national half marathon had a record of 1:03.46. Avinash was confident of his physical fitness and his capability of winning a medal at the Olympics.

Just as with athletes all over the world, COVID-19 took a heavy toll on Avinash too. The lack of training and competition was a major concern. At the 2020 Tokyo Olympics held later in July 2021, Avinash set a national record of 8:18.12. He finished 7th in his heat but could not make it to the finals. It was a major setback for him.

But he picked himself up. In 2022, he broke his own national record for the seventh time, and in the Rabat Diamond League leg, which took place in June, Avinash clocked 8:17.18 to enter the top 10.

In the 2022 World Athletics Championships in Eugene, USA, Avinash clocked 8:31.75 and ended up 11th in the finals. It nearly broke him. The setback added to his determination and Sable got hungrier to perform better. He was determined to prove himself in the forthcoming 2022 Commonwealth Games in Birmingham. He practised hard, and the results were there for all to see. At first, he trailed at number 4 behind the Kenyans, till the last 500 metres. He had put in his best, with a timing of 8:11.20. It was the ninth time he bettered his own national record in the 3000-metre steeplechase. He had been aiming for the gold, and was confident about winning it, but missed it by 0.05 seconds. Abraham Kibiwot of Kenya beat him to take the gold. Avinash had to settle for silver. However, it was still a momentous victory as it was the first time since the 1994 Commonwealth Games that a non-Kenyan had won a medal. Avinash ended Kenya's long dominance in the 3000-metre steeplechase event.

Sable had wanted to prove that it was not just the Africans—Kenyans and Ethiopians—who could win in long-distance races. An Indian could win too.

In the 19th Asian Games at Hangzhou in 2023, Avinash was unstoppable as he went on to win one medal after another. He won a gold medal in the 3000-metre men's steeplechase final. He recorded a timing of 8:19.50. It was an enormous achievement for the man from Mandwa. Not content with the win, Avinash clinched a silver in the men's 5000 metre. It was his second medal at the Asian Games. He aims to blaze new records in the 2024 Paris Olympics.

Though not aware of the importance of his medals or his goals, Avinash's parents are justifiably proud of their son, who is famously called 'Silver Sable' by many.

> In 2022, Avinash Sable won a silver, becoming the first non-Kenyan person since 1994 to win a medal at the Commonwealth Games.

He also dreams of starting an academy back home to support young talent and train them early on.

Eldhose Paul: The Man with a Golden Leap

The Story

Eldhose Paul was born on 7 November 1996 in Kolenchery, a small village in Ernakulum in Kerala. His father, Kochuthottathil Paulose, worked as a daily wage labourer, and mother, Mariyakutty was a homemaker. The family lived in dire financial crisis, amidst which little Eldhose lost his mother. Eldhose was just four years old then. Realizing that Paulose could not look after his sons, the children's grandmother, Maryamma, stepped in and took charge of them.

It was difficult for a woman of Maryamma's age to bring up two small children. Poverty didn't make it any easier. Yet, she did her best to bring up the two boys. Eldhose's brother, Abin Paul, was often unwell too. Thus, Eldhose had little choice. At an early age, he took up any work that came his way. From rubber tapping to tiling roofs, he did it all so he could earn some money.

The Journey

It was after joining Krishnan Elayath Memorial High School in Alangad that Eldhose started taking some interest in sports. He concentrated on athletics with the belief that excellence in sports would lead him to employment and that their struggles would be over. He tried his hand at pole vaulting before switching to triple jumps. His aim was to get admission in the sports hostel at Mar Athanasius College (MAC) after passing his class 12 because the college was well known for its success in grooming sportspersons from the region.

MAC was also known for its sports coach, T.P. Ouseph, a former Indian Air Force athlete, who has groomed several national and international champions like S. Murali, Bobby Aloysius and Anju Bobby George. Eldhose was desperate to train under Ouseph, whom he considered his passport to success. At first, Ouseph rejected him because Eldhose was 5 feet 8 inches. The average height of national and international triple jumpers is 6 feet. Thus, the coach felt that Eldhose was too short for the triple jump.

> While the average height of national and international triple jumpers is 6 feet, Eldhose Paul was 5 feet 8 inches.

Eldhose was dejected. However, he refused to wallow in self-pity. Instead, the rejection spurred Eldhose to do better and he started working diligently to improve his personal mark.

The hard work paid off when Ouseph observed Eldhose's speed, flexible body and energy. He decided to give the hardworking teenager the chance he deserved. That was the turning point in Eldhose's life.

When he was brought to Ouseph, Eldhose could jump around 13 metres high; the next year he improved to 14 metres, and by the third year, he was jumping nearly 16 metres.

At that time, Eldhose was struggling with financial problems, so he worked in his grandmother's saw mill during the weekends. He faced all challenges stoically.

Things seemed to change for the better as Eldhose secured a job with the Indian Navy in 2016. Not only would the job take the family out of a financial morass, but it would also shape Eldhose's sporting career. That was the beginning of his excellence. He had been jumping as high as 15.75 metres, but he scored 16 metres after training for a while. His target was to improve his personal mark, and he worked diligently towards that goal.

Eldhose's dedication and single-minded approach towards his goal soon paid off. He won a gold medal at the Services meet. In 2019, the medal brought his competence to the fore, and he was noticed. Not only was he selected for the nationals, but he was also placed under coach M. Harikrishnan, who competed in the long jump event for India at the 2010 Commonwealth Games (CWG) in New Delhi.

It was a given that Eldhose would improve his personal mark under the guidance of Harikrishnan, whose personal best was 7.92 metres in the long jump. In 2016, the coach had hung up his spikes to join a coaching programme at NSNIS, Patiala. Harikrishnan designed a specific programme for Eldhose to suit his body structure. He not only had to correct his technical flaws but also learn to give his best even at 5 feet 8 inches.

Triple jump involves making a horizontal jump for distance using a hop, which requires the athlete to take off and land on the same foot; a step, in which the athlete lands on the other foot; and finally, a jump, which involves landing in any manner, usually by making use of both feet together. Perfection in the three results in a medal. Harikrishnan found that Eldhose's running style needed improvement. A triple jumper must not run with legs wide open, which was proving to be Eldhose's undoing.

Harikrishnan designed several workouts and used a resistance band to help Eldhose maintain the required distance between his legs while running. Harikrishnan also trained him to straighten his upper body, which tended to lag while running.

Under Harikrishnan's guidance, Eldhose began crossing the 16-metre mark. It was an enormous leap towards his goal.

Eldhose won the national championships held in Patiala in 2021. His most striking performance resulted in him clinching the gold medal in three Indian Grand Prix athletics events.

The year 2022 proved to be a promising one for the triple jumper. He would compete in foreign lands for the first time. The first one in a series of competitions was the one in Almaty, Kazakhstan, where he won a silver and qualified for the World Athletics Championships to be held in Eugene.

It was an opportunity to prove himself, but there were innumerable hurdles. Paul encountered visa issues and could only manage to be cleared for travel just a day before the start of the competition. To compound his problems, Harikrishnan's visa didn't arrive in time for him to travel to Eugene.

At Eugene, Eldhose was competing against the best triple jumpers, and he was doing so without the support and motivation of his coach. But it proved to be an enormous learning experience for the young man. He benefitted by watching the top triple jumpers as they trained and competed.

His absence didn't prevent coach Harikrishnan from guiding Eldhose over video calls. The two triple jumpers, Eldhose and Abdulla Aboobacker, who were training under Harikrishnan, sent him videos of their practice.

Although Eldhose ranked 9th in the World Championship, it was a commendable achievement for him. He became the first Indian to qualify for the triple jump final at the World Championship.

At the 2022 Commonwealth Games in Birmingham, both Eldhose and Aboobacker created a sensation when they bagged the gold and silver medals respectively in the triple jump. It was a double whammy for India when Eldhose, who had struggled to cross the 17-metre mark initially, leaped to create a personal best of 17.03 metres. His hard work and determination helped India win its first-ever gold in the men's triple jump at the Commonwealth Games.

> Eldhose Paul was the first Indian to win a gold medal in the men's triple jump event at the Commonwealth Games 2022 in Birmingham.

Back home in Kolencherry, the villagers were jubilant. Their boy had brought honour to the village and the country.

During the qualifying event for the Asian Games in Hangzhou, Eldhose secured the gold medal, but he fell short of the 16.60-metre entry mark set by the AFI for the Asian Games. He fell short of the qualifying mark in the 2023 World Championships in Budapest, making it a disappointing year for Eldhose.

1st Indian to win GOLD at the World Athletics U20 2018

Hima Das

ATHLETICS

Hima Das: The Dhing Express

The Story

On 9 January 2000, Hima was born in a rice farmer's house in the small village of Kandhulimari located on the eastern edge of the Brahmaputra in Assam. The place is near Dhing town, which is why Hima is nicknamed the 'Dhing Express'. She is the oldest of five children and lives in a big extended family of 18 members.

Hima was always a fearless child. Sometimes it would disturb her mother when her father allowed her to do whatever she wanted. There was a time when she raced against a Tata Sumo during her school days and won.

One day when Hima was returning from school, which was just a short distance away, a car came to a halt next to her. Her friends, who were accompanying her at the time, were offered a ride while she was left out. In a fit of anger at being refused, Hima challenged the driver and emerged victorious in the race to her home.

The Journey

Hima, like the other children in her village, aspired to become a professional footballer. In the past, her dad too had played football, which sparked her interest in the sport.

Golden Sportspersons

> As a child, Hima aspired to become a professional footballer. She became skilled at the game and even played in inter-club and inter-village matches.

She joined the village boys in playing football and became skilled at the game. She played in both inter-club and inter-village matches. Players would receive either 500 or 1000 rupees for participating. Hima would save the money thus earned.

She ran freely and swiftly, outpacing the boys on uneven, muddy football fields.

She made a habit of running in the field before dawn and after dusk, since the cattle grazed there during the day. Hima, always willing to work hard, assisted her father in ploughing the paddy field and transporting the harvest on a bicycle.

Hima created a group of local friends called Mon Jai, her favourite phrase in Assamese. The goal of the group was to help people. Thus, she led a group of women to oppose the local vendor selling country liquor. When the vendor disregarded their advice about selling alcohol, they reacted by demolishing his shop and smashing the bottles.

Shamsul Haque was the one who discovered Hima's potential as an athlete. He worked as a physical education teacher at Hima's school, Jawahar Navodaya Vidyalaya. He noticed Hima's ability to be a good sprinter and encouraged her to pursue it.

His words prompted Hima to think about a career in sports, and thus, she consented to train for the local racing events. Haque's training resulted in an improvement in her running skills. She was now serious about her athletic dream and recognized the need for professional training. There were some obstacles to her dream. Dhing

Hima Das: The Dhing Express

lacked sporting infrastructure, and during monsoons, the grounds would submerge in water.

Hima's outstanding performance at an inter-district event caught the attention of Nipon Das, a trainer with the state Directorate of Sports and Youth Welfare. He convinced her parents that her athletic future was promising and suggested sending her to Guwahati for training with a professional coach.

Initially, Hima's parents were hesitant about sending her away, but she managed to persuade them. Ronjit Das, her father, gave Hima 400 rupees for the expenses.

Nipon Das and another coach, Nabajit Malakar, got a house on rent for her. In addition, they had made arrangements for her food, but she felt disoriented. Adjusting to city life can be challenging for a girl who grew up in a village surrounded by family and friends. However, Hima exhibited nothing of her uncertainty before her family. Instead, she assured them of her confidence to deal with things.

> At the Federation Cup in Patiala, Hima sprinted across the finish line in a remarkable 51.97 seconds, qualifying for the Commonwealth Games.

From winning medals in state-level competitions to national-level ones, Hima travelled the distance in a short time. In March 2018, at the Federation Cup in Patiala, Hima Das sprinted across the finish line in a remarkable 51.97 seconds to clinch the gold medal in the 400-metre race. It was a noteworthy feat that broke the 52-second qualifying mark for the upcoming Commonwealth Games.

She was now ready for international podiums. Hima was thus a part of the Indian contingent that participated in the 2018 Commonwealth Games held in Gold Coast, Australia. While Hima's specialty was the 100- and 200-metre sprints, in Australia, she participated in the 400-metre sprint and finished in the 6th position.

She won a gold at the IAAF World U20 Championships in Finland in the 400-metre event by clocking 51.46 seconds. She became the first Indian track athlete to win a gold at any track event at the World Athletics Championships, junior or senior, and the second Indian to win gold (the first was Neeraj Chopra for javelin in 2016). Impressed by her performance, Galina Bukharina, the famous Russian athlete and coach, agreed to take Hima under her wing.

In Jakarta, Hima continued her winning spree as she won a silver medal at the 2018 Asian Games, setting a national record with a time of 50.79 seconds in the 400-metre individual event. She was also part of the women's relay and mixed relay teams at the Asian Games. The team won two gold medals. Interestingly, this was the first time that a mixed relay was held.

Hima's success was no flash in the pan. She went on to win five consecutive gold medals in 2019. The first was a gold medal won at the Poznan Athletics Grand Prix in Poland, and then a second victory at the Kutnos Athletics Meet, again in Poland. She won the third gold at the Kladno Athletics Meet, the fourth gold at Tabor Athletics Meet and, finally, the fifth at Mezinarodni Mitink, all three of which were held in the Czech Republic. In a brief span of 19 days, Hima had won five gold medals.

Life came full circle for Hima—the young girl who once used to scribble a popular brand name on her running shoes went on to clinch an endorsement deal with the same brand. Hima was honoured with the Arjuna Award, the second-highest sporting award in the country, in a glittering ceremony at the Rashtrapati Bhavan, New Delhi, on 25 September 2018.

Hima was also appointed India's first-ever youth ambassador by UNICEF.

On 26 February 2021, Hima was appointed as Deputy Superintendent of Assam Police.

Hima's success results from many sleepless nights of running alone on the tracks. It is the fruit of consistent hard work and self-belief.

Murali Sreeshankar: The Giant Leaper

The Story

Murali Sreeshankar was born on 27 March 1999 in a family of athletes in the Palakkad district of Kerala. His father, S. Murali, is a former triple jumper who won a silver medal at the South Asian Games, and his mother, K.S. Bijimol, is also an athlete who won a silver medal in 800 metres at the 1992 Asian Junior Athletics Championship. With his cousins being tennis and basketball players, it was a given that Sreeshankar would take up sports one day.

When Sreeshankar was just 4 years of age, he often accompanied his father to his practice. The little boy too would run and jump about while his father continued his athletics practice. During this time, his father noticed the boy as he ran, and realized that his son had the potential to become a good sprinter. S. Murali began guiding the boy and soon the two of them were practising together.

S. Murali would tell his son stories about great players like Carl Lewis and important Indian athletes to motivate Sreeshankar. His mother used to train with Shiny Wilson, who often visited their house and narrated interesting stories about her career. These stories had a great effect on the little boy. Sreeshankar ran whenever he could. He jumped vigorously on the sofa and on the bed, often damaging the furniture. Like his parents and cousins, Sreeshankar wanted to be an athlete too.

The result of his determination soon showed as Sreeshankar started winning racing competitions with other boys. He took part in the 50-metre and 100-metre sprint in the Under-10 category and became the state champion. It didn't take long for the father, a formidable sportsperson himself, to realize that his son would make a good long jumper.

The Journey

Sreeshankar switched from sprints to long jump at the age of 13, and by the time he reached class 10, he was training seriously to be a long jumper. He began taking significant leaps in the sport under his father's coaching, who had trained under foreign coaches and knew how to develop an athlete properly.

At the National Open Athletics Championships in 2018 in Bhubaneswar, the 19-year-old Sreeshankar made history by breaking the men's long jump national record with an incredible jump of 8.20 metres, earning himself a gold medal. It was a promising start in his journey.

Unlike some sportspersons, Sreeshankar did not give up his studies to pursue sports full-time. He was good at studies, just as he was at sports. After finishing his school at the Kendriya Vidyalaya, Sreeshankar applied for medical and engineering entrance exams and cracked both. His NEET scores would have got him a seat in any medical college in Kerala.

Sreeshankar was in a dilemma. Although it would ensure a secure future, opting for medicine would shift his entire attention to academics and he would have no time for athletics. So, instead of opting for medicine, he enrolled at the NSS College of Engineering, Palakkad. But he soon realized that engineering required long and intensive study hours. It would leave him little time for his sport. So, he started studying B.Sc. (Mathematics) at Government Victoria College, Palakkad.

In 2017, Sreeshankar showed remarkable improvement in his performance under the guidance of his father. With a height of 5 feet 9 inches and a weight of 65 kilograms, he was well-suited for long jumps.

His father would coach him, training him in the synthetic track stadium of the Government Medical College, Palakkad. It was a simple one, with no dressing rooms or washrooms. A shed with aluminium sheets served as a makeshift gym and changing room.

In March 2018, Sreeshankar cleared 7.99 metres and qualified for the 2018 Commonwealth Games but had to miss the event due to a surgery.

In the meantime, the AFI got a retired Romanian triple jumper, Bedros Bedrosian, to train Indian athletes, especially for jumps. The AFI moved the national camp for jumps from Trivandrum to Palakkad to facilitate Sreeshankar's training there so Sreeshankar could continue his studies uninterrupted. However, things didn't go as planned. Bedros Bedrosian was not happy with the facilities and resigned. Sreeshankar was also reluctant to train under any coach other than his father.

Nevertheless, 2018 was an eventful year for Sreeshankar. During the Federation Cup in Patiala in March that year, he cleared 7.99 metres and qualified to represent India at the 2018 Commonwealth

Games to be held in April at Gold Coast, Australia. Unfortunately, 10 days before the games, he was diagnosed with appendicitis and had to undergo emergency surgery. By the time he returned home, he had lost considerable weight and had difficulty moving around. Thus, he missed the 2018 Commonwealth Games.

Sreeshankar recovered under the watchful eye of the doctors and two months later, in June, he competed in the 2018 Asian Junior Athletics Championships at Gifu, Japan, winning a bronze medal with a leap of 7.47 metres. In August 2018, at the Asian Games in Jakarta, he did better with a jump of 7.95 metres but was placed 6th in the finals. Back home, he broke the national record with a jump of 8.20 metres at the National Open Athletics Championships in Bhubaneswar in September 2018.

With his record-breaking jump at Bhubaneswar, Sreeshankar qualified for the 2019 World Athletic Championships, which were scheduled to begin in September 2019 in Doha.

However, Sreeshankar sustained a heel injury, causing him to take a break lasting months, which kept him away from the field.

Finally fit, in the run-up to the World Championships, he won gold medals at the March 2019 Grand Prix Athletics Championships, Punjab, and at the Tatyana Kolpakova International Athletics in Bishkek, Kyrgyzstan, in July. Unfortunately, he failed to qualify for the finals at the 2019 World Championships in Doha. Despite previously jumping 8.20 metres in Bhubaneswar, Sreeshankar fell short with a 7.62-metre jump in the heats, where the qualifying mark was set at 8.15 metres.

The pandemic created havoc all around the world. Eager for him to get back into shape for the Olympics, after the COVID-19 lockdown was lifted, Sreeshankar's parents bought a piece of land close to their house so they could buy some equipment and set up a gym.

The Federation Cup Senior National Athletics Championships were scheduled to be held in Patiala from 15–19 March 2021. This served as the qualifier for Olympic Games, Tokyo. Sreeshankar competed and, with a leap of 8.26 metres, secured his Olympics berth for the 2020 Tokyo Olympics. The Olympic qualification mark was 8.22 metres. Although he qualified for the Tokyo Olympics, Sreeshankar fared poorly at the fitness trials just before the Olympics, and the AFI wanted to drop his name from the Olympic squad. It was heartbreaking for him and his family, who were looking forward to his participation in the Olympic Games. In the end, his father gave a written submission, committing that Sreeshankar would produce at least the qualification performance at the Olympics. The officials finally allowed Sreeshankar to proceed to Tokyo.

Sreeshankar, however, could not perform as well as he had expected. He had expected to qualify for the finals, but his best jump was far below expectations. The jump of 7.69 metres was not good enough to help Sreeshankar qualify for the finals. He stood 13th in the heats.

The poor performance drew brickbats the moment Sreeshankar returned from Tokyo. The criticism from various quarters was disappointing. Things got worse when the AFI, which had not been in favour of sending him for the Olympics, took a serious view of his performance and decided to remove his father from training him further and brought in a new coach instead. But S. Murali continued to train his son alongside the new coach, Volker Herrmann, appointed by the AFI.

After Volker Herrmann quit, a new foreign coach, Russian Denis Kapustin, the 2000 Sydney Olympics triple jump bronze medallist, coached Sreeshankar at the national camp in Bengaluru. There was a marked improvement in Sreeshankar's performance. In March 2022, he set a new national record at the World Indoor Championships in Belgrade, Serbia, with a jump of 7.92 metres in his third attempt and finished 7th.

In April 2022, at the Federation Cup Senior Athletics Championships at Kozhikode, Jeswin Aldrin beat Tokyo Olympian Sreeshankar with a jump of 8.37 metres. Both qualified for the world championships.

In May 2022, he won the gold with a leap of 8.31 metres at the 12th International Jumping Meeting in Kallithea, Greece.

In July 2022, Sreeshankar qualified for the finals at the World Athletics Championships in Oregon. Although his leap of 7.96 metres was lower than the 8.15-metre qualifying mark, he qualified for the finals since he was in the first 12. With this, he became the first Indian to do so in the long jump. However, in the finals, he was a disappointing 7th.

Sreeshankar silenced his detractors with his stupendous performance in the finals during the long jump event of the 2022 Commonwealth Games in Birmingham. It was his first appearance at the Commonwealth Games, but that didn't stop him from winning a silver medal with his leap of 8.08 metres. With that medal, he became the first Indian to win a silver in long jump.

There was jubilation in the country. The hard work of his father, and the faith of his family, had stood him in good stead.

> At the 2022 Commonwealth Games in Birmingham, Sreeshankar became the first Indian to win a silver medal in long jump.

The celebrations had not fully died down after this win when Sreeshankar faced another challenge at the Monaco Diamond League 2022. He failed to clear the 8-metre mark and finished 6th with a jump of 7.94 metres.

However, the best was still to come. Sreeshankar kept his head up and worked towards keeping his game strong. Thus, at the Asian Games 2023, Sreeshankar secured a silver medal, jumping an impressive 8.19 metres high.

Recognizing his remarkable performance in athletics, the Government of India presented Sreeshankar with the Arjuna Award in January 2024.

Winning an Olympic medal has been Sreeshankar's dream for the longest time. Being picked for the Indian team propelled him closer to his goal. However, a knee injury sustained during training shattered Sreeshankar's dream, who will sadly have to give the Paris 2024 games a miss.

1ST INDIAN to win a GOLD at the WORLD CHAMPIONSHIP

NEERAJ Chopra

ATHLETICS

Neeraj Chopra: The Man with the Midas Touch

The Story

Neeraj Chopra was born on 24 December 1997 to a couple in a small village called Khandra in Haryana. Like many in the village, his father, Satish Kumar Chopra, is a farmer. The eldest among the siblings, Neeraj grew up in a joint family of 19 members.

Neeraj was a mischievous child. He fiddled with the beehives on the trees and pulled buffaloes by their tails. Once, while trying to drive away bees from a nearby tree, he accidentally set fire to a part of his house. There was an unending series of such mischiefs.

Neeraj was dearly loved and pampered with a diet rich in fat and sugar, a common practice in North Indian households. As a result, Neeraj became an overweight child. At 11, he weighed 90 kilograms and was teased by his peers.

The Journey

It was then that Satish Chopra decided that his son needed to lose weight. He wanted Neeraj to be occupied with something that would help him shed weight and teach him to be disciplined.

Neeraj's *chacha* (paternal uncle) always insisted that he take up sports. He even asked Neeraj to choose between sports and studies and, assuming that his uncle would be proud of the choice he made, Neeraj would pick studies, pretending to like studying over anything else. Quite the mischief-monger! However, his uncle was never convinced with Neeraj's quick-witted responses and continued to motivate him to take up sports.

One morning, Neeraj's father took him to Shivaji Stadium in Panipat, which is about 14 kilometres from Khandra. He simply went there to lose weight.

There were a lot of sports at the stadium, but Neeraj saw his seniors throwing javelin—he enjoyed watching it go very far and get stuck in the ground. He felt like he wanted to do the same. One day, at a senior's bidding, Chopra tried to throw the javelin himself.

It was the year 2010, and the 13-year-old Neeraj had no training in javelin throw. Yet, he hurled the javelin to a distance of 40 metres. His throw impressed Jaiveer, and the javelin thrower took the boy under his wing. But Jaiveer soon left for Jalandhar, and Neeraj's practice came to a halt. By now, he was serious about his training. So, at 14, Neeraj moved to Panchkula, where he practised on a synthetic track at Tau Devi Lal Sports Complex for the first time and trained under coach Naseem Ahmad.

Once Neeraj began practising, there was no looking back. Jan Zelezny, the world record holder and greatest javelin thrower of all time, became his idol. He downloaded videos of the Czech champion and attempted to copy his style of throwing the javelin.

At 15, Neeraj could hurl the javelin to over 60 metres, which was a feat in itself. By now, confident of his success, Neeraj began preparing for the 2012 National Junior Athletics Championships to be held in Lucknow. There, he won his first gold and set a new national record with a throw of 68.46 metres. This drew the attention of sports authorities. They felt he was ready to take part in international competitions.

In 2013, Neeraj took part in his first international athletics event held in Donetsk, Ukraine, at the IAAF World Youth Championships. Neeraj, however, couldn't win any medal and finished 19th in the qualifiers.

In the meantime, he suffered a wrist fracture and had to stop practising for almost six months. This added to his disappointment.

In just two months, his weight shot up to 93 kilograms. It was a matter of concern, so he began training to lose the excess weight. Neeraj also had to practise for the Youth Nationals, which would pave the way for selection in the World Youth Games. It took him four months of hard work to lose nearly 10 kilograms.

In 2014, his hard work paid off as Neeraj won a silver medal in the Bangkok Youth Olympics Qualification. The medal proved to be a morale booster as it was his first ever at an international platform, and he began training harder.

The year 2016 was a breakthrough for Neeraj as he bagged a gold medal at the South Asian Games in Guwahati with a throw of 82.23 metres. The Indian Army recruited him in the rank of Naib Subedar. He won a gold medal in the IAAF World U20 Championships in Bydgoszcz, Poland, by setting a world junior record of 86.48 metres.

The list of Neeraj's firsts is long and enviable. He is the first Indian track and field athlete to set a world record and win the championship in the World U20 Championships 2016, and the first Indian javelin thrower to win a gold medal in the 2018 Asian Games in Jakarta.

Winning a medal in the Olympic Games is every athlete's dream. It was Neeraj's dream too. Just as he began preparing for the Rio Olympics, he sustained a back injury in April 2016 during the

Federation Cup in New Delhi, which severely impacted his preparation for the Olympics. As a result, Neeraj could not throw over the 83-metre mark at the pre-Olympics camp in Poland and didn't qualify for the 2016 Rio Olympics. He also suffered an elbow injury in his right arm, due to which he missed the 2019 Doha World Championships. So, in May 2019, he underwent an arthroscopic surgery in Mumbai, ironically on the same day that the qualification window for Tokyo opened.

> Neeraj Chopra became the first Indian track and field athlete to win an Olympic gold medal at the Tokyo Olympics in 2021 after a 100-year wait.

Neeraj had been away from competitions for nearly eight months because of this injury. But it was sheer determination that saw him bounce back from what could have been a long hiatus. He travelled to South Africa to train with the biomechanics expert Dr Klaus Bartonietz, and the two of them worked tirelessly to get him back in shape. In January 2020, he returned to competitive action and qualified for the Tokyo Olympics.

But his resilience was put to test yet again when COVID-19 hit, and the Tokyo Olympics got postponed to 2021. The nation was looking forward to witnessing some of its best sportspersons compete at the world platform. Neeraj lived up to everyone's dream. Indians will not forget his superlative performance, which finally ended India's 100-year wait for an Olympic gold medal in athletics.

He was also awarded the Major Dhyan Chand Khel Ratna Award in 2021. The Army Sports Institute Stadium in Pune was renamed the Neeraj Chopra Stadium in honour of the Olympian's unparalleled victory.

He went on to become the first Indian to win a silver medal at the World Athletics Championships 2022 in Oregon, and the first Indian to win a Diamond League Meeting in Lausanne 2022. On 9 September 2022, the Indian javelin star scripted history once again in Zurich when he became the first Indian Diamond League Champion.

In the Asian Games 2023 at Hangzhou, Neeraj Chopra lived up to the nation's expectations and claimed the gold in men's javelin throw with a throw of 88.88 metres. On 10 May 2024, Neeraj won a silver medal in the Doha Diamond League with a throw of 88.36 metres followed by a gold in the men's javelin throw event five days later at the Federation Cup 2024 in Bhubaneswar, Odisha. He recorded a throw of 82.27 metres.

Success followed him everywhere he went. Many brands and establishments wanted to bring him on board.

He was awarded the Arjuna Award in 2018, and the army promoted him to the rank of Subedar.

In 2020, he was given the Vishisht Seva Medal.

In 2022, he was awarded the Param Vishisht Seva Medal and the Padma Shri, the fourth-highest civilian award.

With each medal, the expectations continue to grow. The nation has now set its eyes on the 2024 Paris Olympics.

> Neeraj Chopra has been awarded the Padma Shri, the Arjuna Award, the Vishisht Seva Medal and the Param Vishisht Seva Medal over the years.

1st Indian Woman to Win Asiad Gold

Heptathlon 2018

Swapna Barman

ATHLETICS

Swapna Barman: The Heptathlon Star

The Story

Swapna Barman's story is one of hunger, struggle and resilience. She was born to a very poor family on 29 October 1996 in a small village called Ghoshpara in Jalpaiguri, West Bengal. Her father, Panchanan Barman, was a rickshaw puller and her mother worked in a tea garden. The couple, who lived in a thatched house with a tin shed for a roof, could barely afford a couple of meals a day when Swapna was born. She was the fourth child.

When she was 11, Panchanan heard that an athlete who won some competitions could get a job. So, he encouraged his daughter to become an athlete. Thus, Swapna began training for high jumps. Her father gave her a ride in his rickshaw to the stadium, which was some distance from their home. Ignoring her painful toes, she continued to practice. (Interestingly, Swapna was born with six toes on each foot!)

The turning point in her life arrived when she began training under Sukanta Sinha, a former athlete. He noticed the determination in her and encouraged her to practise high jumps.

Disaster fell on the family when Panchanan had a stroke. He became bedridden, and the family lost the little money he used to earn. Basana Devi, Swapna's mother, worked harder by taking up more work as a household help, along with her work in the tea garden.

At that time, Swapna had not heard of Asian Games or any other international sporting event. All she knew was that a medal could get her a job and it would help the family. Athletes need good, nutritious food, but food was scarce in the Barman house. There were no equipment or training grounds in the village.

Swapna practised high jumps using a temporary bamboo structure made by her father, which helped her win several local competitions. Swapna's fame reached Subhash Sarkar, an athlete who had switched to being a coach. He too was a resident of Jalpaiguri. Sarkar had been told that Swapna had just won a medal in the Under-14 school nationals in high jump. Curiosity piqued, the Sports Authority of India (SAI) coach wasted no time and headed straight to Ghoshpara village. To his astonishment, he discovered Swapna diligently practising high jump on the bamboo structure her father had built before falling ill.

> In the absence of proper facilities, Swapna practised high jumps using a temporary bamboo structure that was made by her father.

The coach, who had several years of experience, noticed the girl's skill and mental toughness, and that was when Swapna's real training began. Her mother faithfully took her to the Jalpaiguri Sports Complex every day, where Sarkar trained her with unwavering dedication. In 2011, Sarkar took Swapna to the SAI's Kolkata complex. Soon, he became her coach and began training her for the heptathlon.

The Journey

In Kolkata, Swapna faced a lot of ridicule because of her fitness levels. However, under Subhas Sarkar's guidance, Swapna started training for the heptathlon. Many detractors thought he was wasting his time over Swapna. They said she was too short and did not have the right physique for the sport. Additionally, having 12 toes posed a significant challenge for the athlete aspiring to compete in the heptathlon.

Swapna's major hurdle was to find a pair of shoes that could fit her extra toes. She could not afford a good pair of shoes, so getting a customized one was out of the question. Most heptathletes use seven pairs of shoes for each of the different events, and Swapna didn't have a single good pair.

Practising with regular shoes was painful, but she didn't complain. Concerned about his pupil's condition, Sarkar sought help from all quarters, relying on allopathy, Ayurveda and acupuncture to relieve her of the constant pain, but nothing worked. He also tried everything possible, from medicine to exercise, to help her gain height.

At 17, she became the youngest competitor in heptathlon at the 2014 Asian Games held in Incheon, South Korea. She came 5th, with an impressive score of 5,178, despite the discomfort of wearing two pairs of shoes that were too narrow for her six-toed feet. It is common for heptathletes to have a minimum of four pairs of shoes to participate in all seven disciplines.

It was a landmark year for Swapna because she was noticed by Rahul Bose, actor and former rugby player. He helped her apply for their GoSports athlete mentorship programme that offered her unwavering support in her sporting journey.

In 2015, she returned home after an injury while training at the SAI. She suffered many injuries and setbacks, but those didn't stop her from competing.

The Asian Games were close, which offered little time for her injuries to heal. Things took a turn for the worse when Swapna suffered a spine injury.

Despite the doctor's advice to rest her spine and get herself operated, she continued her training while relying on physiotherapy. Neither her doctor nor her physiotherapist or coach was hopeful of Swapna winning a medal. However, she bagged a gold at the 2017 Asian Championships, Bhubaneswar.

Enduring her injuries and pain, Swapna pinned her hopes on winning a medal in the 2018 Asian Games to be held in Jakarta. Accompanied by her coach, she travelled to Jakarta.

In Jakarta, Swapna's sufferings were far from over. On the day of the event, her jaw became swollen from a tooth infection that she had been experiencing. She subsequently developed a fever because of the infection. To make matters worse, her painful jaw made it nearly impossible for her to eat. But she continued to compete with a bandaged jaw.

Every time she landed after a high jump, the swollen jaw was agony for her. Every movement hurt. But Swapna braved the agony and continued with the competition. She had come too far to give up just when she was so close to fulfilling her dream.

Back home in the sleepy hamlet of Ghospara in Jalpaiguri, friends and neighbours assembled in the modest Barman house to watch Swapna's performance on television.

Swapna's perseverance, sincerity and hard work bore her rich rewards when the results were announced and she won India's first heptathlon gold in the Asian Games.

Swapna Barman: The Heptathlon Star

After returning to India, she was honoured with the Arjuna Award. She was also gifted customized footwear by a leading German sportswear brand.

Swapna won the silver medal in heptathlon at the 2019 Asian Athletics Championships in Doha.

Swapna also won a gold medal in high jump at the 2021 National Games held in Warangal. But she also suffered a severe back injury and underwent surgery. The pain, however, refused to go away. There was a time when she contemplated retiring from athletics. However, Swapna's long-time coach, Subhas Sarkar, convinced her to endure the challenges.

Swapna Barman's hard work and perseverance helped her win India's first heptathlon gold in the Asian Games in 2018 in Jakarta.

In 2022, she surprised everyone by making a comeback and winning two gold medals in the National Games in Gujarat. In addition, Swapna achieved a new national record of 1.83 metres in high jump.

Swapna has proved that grit and determination can take one beyond the realms of pain and help one attain the pinnacle of success.

The heptathlete is extremely fond of Kishore Kumar's songs.

Badminton

1. British military officers developed modern badminton in the 1860s in British India from an old children's game of battledore and shuttlecock. It was called Poona because it was very popular in the garrison town of Poona.
2. The British officers took the competitive game back to England. It was officially named Badminton in 1873 at the Badminton House, the Duke of Beaufort's estate in Gloucestershire, England.
3. The Badminton Association of India (BAI) was established in 1899 and is one of the oldest badminton associations in the world.
4. In 1934, The International Badminton Federation (IBF) was established but was later renamed as the Badminton World Federation (BWF). India joined the group in 1936.
5. Prakash Padukone is considered the father of Indian Badminton.
6. A shuttlecock typically weighs between 4.74 and 5.5 grams.
7. There are 16 feathers in a shuttlecock.
8. The maximum permissible length of a badminton racket is 68 centimetres.
9. Players are required to make 21 points in a set to win a game.
10. Badminton was officially included in the Olympic Games in 1992.

GOLD at the COMMONWEALTH GAMES 2022

MEN'S SINGLES

Lakshya Sen

BADMINTON

Lakshya Sen: The Golden Shuttler

The Story

Lakshya Sen was born on 16 August 2001 in Almora, Uttarakhand. He was born with badminton in his genes. His mother, Nirmala, is a high school teacher while his father, Dhirendra Kumar Sen or D.K. Sen, is a national badminton coach at the SAI. Lakshya's brother, Chirag, who is older by three years, is also a national badminton champion. The Sen family has been playing the game for three generations now. Lakshya's paternal grandfather, Chandra Lal Sen, who was a national badminton player, took the little boy along whenever he went to play. It was Chandra Sen who taught the basics of the game to Lakshya.

Inspired by their grandfather and father, the two brothers would play for fun and try to outdo each other, enjoying the game with no pressure. The senior Sens watched and gave them useful tips to improve their game. This helped, and the game between the two young brothers improved considerably. When D.K. Sen began coaching his elder son, Lakshya wanted to be coached, too.

From the beginning, Lakshya was very keen on learning the nitty-gritty of the game. Thus, he started accompanying his brother to various tournaments. In 2010, when he was about 9 years old, he accompanied his father and brother to Bangalore (now Bengaluru), where Chirag was participating in the Under-13 badminton tournament. Chirag did well and won the Under-13 title.

Lakshya was impressed by his brother's victory and wanted to be like him. It was around this time that Prakash Padukone and coach Vimal Kumar, who were scouting for talent, noticed Chirag's potential. Padukone, a former badminton champion and co-founder of the Olympic Gold Quest, had established the Prakash Padukone Badminton Academy (PPBA) to train sportspersons for the Olympics.

Chirag was selected to join the PPBA and Lakshya, impressed by the atmosphere and facilities, also expressed his wish to join the academy. Seeing his earnestness, D.K. Sen requested coach Vimal Kumar to take his younger son into the academy too. The coach, however, felt the 9-year-old boy was too young for the academy. So determined was Lakshya that he asked Vimal Kumar to put him on trial and then decide if he was fit enough to join the academy. His game impressed not only the coach but also Prakash Padukone and they enrolled him.

The PPBA is one of the best training grounds for champions, and Lakshya trained there with the older boys selected to join the Olympic Gold Quest. His stay at the academy was a boon as he learned new techniques and improved his skills and his game. But he was still young and learning to accept defeat. He would cry or withdraw to a corner after losing a game. His adamance to win every game, however, improved his game considerably.

There are several benefits of living in a hilly terrain, such as developing strong leg muscles and improving lung capacity. Blessed with these, Lakshya developed speed and stamina that allowed him to play and work out for long hours without getting exhausted.

At the academy, Lakshya learned to smash very hard and confuse his opponent. Over a period of time, he learned to control his emotions and not reveal them to his opponent. He was no longer the boy who was easily disappointed after losing a match. In 2014, badminton champion Saina Nehwal would often visit the academy to practise with the trainees. Lakshya would also play with her, becoming the only one who could beat her during the practice sessions.

At 10, Lakshya won his first international tournament in Singapore at the Singapore Youth International series.

The Journey

Lakshya had the right setting to take up badminton and his family was reasonably well off. However, while a competitive atmosphere can motivate a player, it can also place a lot of pressure and responsibility on their shoulders. The children of many talented players have not always followed in the footsteps of their parents. Those who do sometimes cannot match up to the parents' achievements. But Lakshya followed the elders in his family and by virtue of sheer determination and hard work, he surpassed them all.

> Lakshya Sen was the only player who could beat Saina Nehwal during a practice session at the Prakash Padukone Badminton Academy in 2014.

Family support is important for players. Many parents do not perceive sports as a career for their children. They want their children to do well in academics, pick up some suitable profession and settle down in life. Lakshya was fortunate that his parents knew that it was possible to have a career in sports. His father quit his job at Almora and shifted to Bangalore so that his children could pursue badminton.

Despite the support, every sportsperson is faced with some struggle, though they must work hard and persevere through it. Every sportsperson sets out to play a tournament with the intent to win it, which can cause players a lot of stress. Also, playing against the best in the world demands a lot of skill and stamina. One must push oneself to the maximum to beat the opponent. This can cause injuries and torn ligaments. Recovery and healing can take a lot of time, during which the players are unable to practise. Apart from physical strength, playing a sport also demands unparalleled mental strength. Losing a game is demoralizing and can affect one's mental well being. The only way to beat that is to accept one's weaknesses as much as one's strength and work on them.

After the Indonesia Open in which Lakshya lost to H.S. Prannoy, he was out of action as he had injured his shoulder. This required him to undergo rehab for about a fortnight. Taking a break can be a disadvantage because it takes time to get back in form to play competitive badminton again. In August 2021, Lakshya failed to qualify for the Indian badminton team, losing in the very first round during the trials due to a stomach infection.

However, Lakshya's hard work at the academy and perseverance despite the challenges reaped rich results, and in the years that followed, he began winning competitions at the national and international level. Lakshya's coaches were not surprised when he won national-level tournaments in the Under-13, Under-17 and Under-19 categories. He won the Under-19 championships at 15 and became the youngest Indian to reach the national men's singles final. Prakash Padukone had achieved this rare feat at 16. After winning a bronze medal in the Asia Junior Championships in 2016, Lakshya swiftly climbed up the ladder to compete at the senior international level. He proved his sceptics wrong by winning the men's singles title at the 2016 India International Series.

According to his coach, Lakshya was unstoppable because he wasn't scared of competition. In 2017, he won two BWF international tournaments—the India International Series and the Eurasian Bulgarian Open Tournament. He was also a runner-up at the Tata Open International Tournament. After storming through the junior championships, he was now breaking through the senior ranks.

In 2018, Lakshya won his first gold medal at the Asia Junior Championships after defeating Thailand's Kunlavut Vitidsarn and also won a bronze medal at the World Junior Championships the same year. 2018 turned out to be a fantastic year for Lakshya. He won a silver medal at the Youth Olympic Games singles and a gold in the mixed team event. He became the youngest Indian shuttler to qualify for the World Tour Finals.

Then, he won the Dutch Open and followed it up by winning his first BWF World Tour title in 2019. His kitty of medals was overflowing. In the brief span of his international career, the teenager impressed everyone with his passion, grit and dedication, which led to him winning many medals. In 2019, Lakshya achieved a significant milestone in his badminton career as he broke into the top 50 of the world rankings for the first time, impressing everyone with his scintillating performances. The 18-year-old prodigy from Almora began aiming higher with each passing day. He had learned to use speed as a weapon against his opponents.

Since childhood, Lakshya's aim has been to play in the Olympics. But his back injury spoiled his chances to play in the 2020 Tokyo Olympics. However, Lakshya witnessed a silver lining when the Olympics gold medal winner Viktor Axelsen invited five young shuttlers to train with him in Dubai. Lakshya was one of them. He got the once-in-a-lifetime opportunity to observe how Axelsen managed his own training at the new training base, with no federation or major support structure around him. In those two weeks of partnering with Axelsen, Lakshya learned many invaluable lessons which paid rich dividends in the tournaments that followed.

In 2021, he became the youngest Indian to make it to the BWF World Tour finals, which is a challenging arena with the top eight shuttlers in the world. Lakshya won the bronze medal after he was defeated by fellow Indian Kidambi Srikanth in the semi-finals of the BWF World Championships.

By 2021, his ranking reached its best. From 104 in 2019, he climbed to 19 in just two years and that's a tremendous achievement.

In 2022, at the prestigious All England Open, he ended up as runner-up and notched up a significant climb by improving his world rank to number 9. It was a historic win on many counts. Pullela Gopichand had been the last Indian to bring home the All England trophy in 2001.

> In May 2022, Lakshya played a winning game and clinched the Thomas Cup. It was a historic win for India—the first ever in 73 years.

2022 saw Lakshya score a few other important victories. In May 2022, he played a winning game and clinched the Thomas Cup for India. It was the first Thomas Cup won by the country in 73 years. While on his way to Bangkok, he suffered food poisoning, but that didn't prevent him from putting up a brave fight for the gold medal in the tournament.

At the 2022 Commonwealth Games in Birmingham, he brought home the much-coveted gold medal.

In July 2023, Lakshya Sen claimed his second BWF Super 500 title in the Canada Open final against China's Li Shi Feng. This was Sen's first title since his victory at the Commonwealth Games in August 2022.

On 1 October 2023, Lakshya Sen was a part of the men's badminton team that won their first-ever silver medal in the men's team championships at the Asian Games 2023.

One reason for Lakshya's phenomenal success is his willingness to learn and adapt. His intensity and the desire to win make him the champion that he is. In the past few years, he observed and learned critical lessons by playing against senior Indian players like Kidambi Srikanth and H.S. Prannoy, and world champions like Loh Kean Yew, Viktor Axelsen, Anders Antonsen and Lee Zii Jia, in various international tournaments. As a result, Lakshya's game has consistently improved with each tournament. His mental strength also lends him an edge, which is an essential element of a player's psychology. Many players break down after losing a match. It was so with Lakshya during his early years, but now he has conquered that attitude.

Lakshya is a balanced and cheerful young man who loves watching Spiderman movies. An animal lover, he often posts pictures with dogs on social media.

His eyes are now set on the 2024 Paris Olympic Games.

P.V. Sindhu: The Badminton Star

The Story

Pusarla Venkata Sindhu, famous as P.V. Sindhu, was born on 5 July 1995 to P.V. Ramana and Vijaya in Hyderabad. Sports formed an important part of her life. With both her parents being national-level volleyball players and her elder sister, P.V. Divya, also a sportsperson, it was natural for Sindhu to be interested in sports. Her father, who was a part of the Indian volleyball team in the 1986 Asian Games, was an inspiration for the young girl. But she was undecided about taking up volleyball like her parents.

> P.V. Sindhu was deeply inspired by her father P.V. Ramana, who represented India at the 1986 Asian Games, and elder sister P.V. Divya, also a sportsperson.

Then one day, Sindhu watched Pullela Gopichand, who had won the 2001 All England Championships, play badminton. That day, she decided to play badminton. Her parents were happy with her choice and the 8-year-old Sindhu started training under Mir

Mehboob Ali at the badminton court of the Indian Railways Institute in Secunderabad. Sindhu's father, who is an Arjuna Award winner, encouraged his daughter to follow her dream. There was a time when Sindhu had wanted to become a doctor. Once she started playing badminton, she enjoyed it so much that she changed her mind.

The Journey

After practising at the Indian Railways Institute for about a year, Sindhu joined the Pullela Gopichand Badminton Academy for training. It was a tough life for the little girl. The academy was far from her house, and her training sessions had to be fitted with the school hours. Sindhu began working towards her goal at a very early age.

While most children her age spent their time playing, Sindhu put in hours of work in training. She woke up at 3 in the morning, and her father dropped her to the academy on his scooter. After the training, she reached her school by 8.30 to focus on her studies. At 4.30 in the noon, she would return to the academy before going home. The daily routine exhausted the little girl. Thus, Sindhu's parents moved to a house close to the academy, so she would not have to travel the distance to her academy.

The result of her hard work soon began showing. Sindhu swept away gold medals at the All India ranking championships (Under-10 and Under-13 categories), and Sub-Junior Nationals (Under-13 doubles). Then she made her way into the international circuit by winning a bronze medal in the 2009 Sub-Junior Asian Badminton Championships. At 17, she won a gold medal in the 2012 Asian Junior Championships. In 2013, she won her first Grand Prix. In the same year, she won a bronze medal at the World Championships.

Sindhu trained hard to reach where she stands today. Her coach, Pullela Gopichand, is a world-class player and a dedicated trainer. He maintains strict discipline and a demanding routine. Sindhu followed the strict regimen of a controlled diet, exercise and training set by her coach.

One by one, Sindhu continued to trounce her challengers and bag prestigious medals at the World Championships. Sindhu continued her winning streak in the Commonwealth Games in 2014, where she won bronze in women's singles.

Aiming to win a medal at the 2016 Rio Olympic Games, Sindhu and her coach worked hard to devise a strategy for her game. They studied the strengths and weaknesses of her opponents and practised her moves accordingly. Sindhu also made a few sacrifices to focus on her game. She gave up her favourite ice creams and chocolates and kept away from her phone and iPad for three full months.

Finally, Sindhu faced her opponents in Rio. She won against the second-seeded Wang Yihan and Japanese star Nozomi Okuhara in the quarter-final and semi-final, respectively. However, in the finals she lost to Spain's Carolina Martin. Nonetheless, her silver medal was a great achievement for India.

On the day of Sindhu's match, her parents and colleagues crowded around the television to watch her play. They cheered at every point she made. There was jubilation, not just in her hometown but all over the country, when she bagged a silver medal after a tough match. With that victory, she became the first and youngest Indian woman athlete to win a silver medal at the Rio Olympics.

Sindhu went on to win silver and gold medals in the singles and mixed team events at the 2018 Commonwealth Games. After two

P.V. Sindhu: The Badminton Star

bronze and two silver medals between 2013 and 2018, she finally won gold in 2019 after comprehensively beating Japan's Nozomi Okuhara 21-7, 21-7 in Basel, Switzerland.

The Indian government awarded her the Arjuna Award and Padma Shri in recognition of her achievements. Forbes listed her as one of the highest-paid female athletes for two consecutive years in 2018 and 2019. She endorsed the products of several prestigious companies.

Sindhu's next target game, the 2020 Tokyo Olympics, was a much-awaited event. It was an exciting match, with the players wanting to grab a medal. With 1.3 billion Indians cheering for her, Sindhu focussed on winning her medal. She emerged victorious in the last 16 against Mia Blichfeldt of Denmark and then went on to defeat Yamaguchi Akane from Japan, the number four seed, in the quarters. P.V. Sindhu defeated China's He Bing Jiao 21-13, 21-15 and returned home with a bronze medal from the 2020 Tokyo Olympic Games. This was her second Olympic medal.

> In November 2022, Sindhu ranked among the top 5 in the women's singles list of the Badminton World Federation. She won her first CWG gold the same year.

A true champion never gives up. Sindhu bounced back with renewed courage each time an opponent defeated her. In November 2022, Sindhu ranked among the top five in the women's singles list of the BWF. She claimed her first Commonwealth Games gold medal in women's singles at the 2022 event in Birmingham. This made her the second women's singles player to win a full set of medals at the Commonwealth Games.

Sindhu now has her sight set on the 2024 Olympic Games to be held in Paris. This time she aims for the gold.

Sindhu, by her own admission, is a foodie and loves all kinds of junk food like ice-creams, biryani, pasta and pizza. But, as is expected, she has to avoid it to keep fit while training for the events. However, after winning a medal, she indulges in everything she loves. Her advice to aspiring athletes is to remain positive and patient and to keep believing in themselves, just like she does.

Her advice to aspiring athletes is to remain positive and patient. Also, to keep believing in themselves, just like she does.

Boxing

1. Ancient Indian texts like Ramayana and Mahabharata contain references to *mushti-yuddha*, which was like boxing. The word 'mushti' stands for fist and 'yuddha' stands for fight.
2. Boxing became a part of the Ancient Greek Olympic Games in 688 BC. Back then, it was a very different kind of competition. Boxers would wrap leather around their hands and forearms to stay safe. There were no time limits for bouts, nor was there a boxing ring. A bout lasted until a participant surrendered.
3. During the 1700s, boxers in England did not wear gloves while fighting.
4. In 1743, Jack Broughton put together the first boxing rules. He is referred to as the Father of Boxing.
5. A set of rules introduced in 1838 made it illegal to kick, bite, head butt or hit below the waist.
6. It was made compulsory for boxers to wear gloves in 1867.
7. Boxing made its official debut in the modern Olympics in 1904 at the St Louis Olympics, USA.
8. Mike Tyson is the youngest boxing heavyweight champion in history.

9. 'The Greatest' is the nickname of Muhammad Ali, the iconic boxer.
10. The USA holds the record for producing the most boxing world champions.
11. It was not until 2001 that the Amateur International Boxing Association (AIBA) started the Women's World Championship, marking serious entry of women into the fray.

Lovlina Borgohain: The Boxing Champion

The Story

Lovlina was born on 2 October 1997 in Tiken and Mamoni Borgohain's humble dwelling in Baromukhia, Assam. She was the third child in their family after twin daughters. The villagers would often express worry for the couple, as they had three daughters and no sons. However, Tiken and Mamoni continued to raise their daughters with a lot of love.

Tiken Borgohain earned just 2,500 rupees by working in a tiny tea estate. It was a small sum for a family of five. Besides other hardships, he could only visit his family for a day every week because the tea estate was far from the village. As a result, Mamoni and the girls began to live by themselves. Concerned about their safety, Mamoni decided that the girls needed to learn self-defence and she enrolled the elder twins, Licha and Lima, in Muay Thai, a type of Thai martial art. Inspired by her sisters, Lovlina also trained in Muay Thai.

Those were difficult times. The three sisters cycled over muddy tracks to Barpathar to learn Muay Thai under coach Prashanta Kumar Das. There was never enough money or food on the table, but Tiken and Mamoni encouraged their daughters to continue with their sporting ambitions. Mamoni took small loans from the village cooperative society to pay for the expenses. This marked the beginning of Lovlina's career in sport.

Muay Thai practice involves using fists, elbows, knees and shins. Lovlina's body was strengthened by practising this martial art for three years and Thang-Ta, a Manipuri martial art, improved her flexibility and agility. She won the Assam championship in Muay Thai and the gold in the national Muay Thai competition. In addition, she secured a silver medal in the Thang-Ta nationals.

> Lovlina Borgohain is trained in the Thai martial arts Muay Thai and Thang-Ta, both of which helped her improve flexibility and agility.

One day, while visiting his family, Tiken Borgohain carried home some sweets wrapped in a newspaper. While she unwrapped the package, Lovlina's attention was caught by Muhammad Ali's picture on the newspaper. Intrigued, she asked her father about the boxer.

Tiken shared the story of the boxer's struggle with poverty and his transformation into a boxing legend. Lovlina found Ali's story fascinating and it sparked a small flame of ambition in her heart.

Soon, destiny took charge. It guided her towards the path that would lead to her success. Lovlina was spotted by Padum Boro, the well-known boxing coach, during a talent hunt. Following his advice, she joined the SAI's boxing training centre in Guwahati in 2012, and the rest is history.

The Journey

Lovlina began her training at the SAI centre in Guwahati, which is over 300 kilometres from Baromukhia. The family was too impoverished to even afford a train ticket for her journey. Things were so bad that both Lovlina and her father had to sleep near the toilet in the train compartment while travelling for the sub-junior nationals. Instead of being demoralized, the challenges served as motivation for her to better her game.

Winning the sub-junior national championship in Kolkata and getting selected for the national camp in Bhopal was a game-changer for Lovlina. In Bhopal, coach Sandhya Gurung took the young girl under her care. Gurung realized Lovlina possessed the qualities for international sports. Her training in Muay Thai and Thang-Ta gave her an edge over the other competitors.

Lovlina possessed ambition, discipline and a strong work ethic. All she needed was to be able to overcome her fear in the ring. It is here that Gurung stepped in and motivated her to believe in herself. It took some time, but Lovlina eventually got the message. She fought in the ring fearlessly, displaying incredible strength and courage.

The training in boxing under Gurung was successful. The Muay Thai training, which requires using both left and right hands, improved her boxing skills. Lovlina won several national and international medals. She won a silver in the 2013 Nations Cup in Serbia, a bronze in the 2017 Asian Championships in Vietnam and a bronze in the 2018 AIBA Women's World Boxing Championships in New Delhi. This was followed by another bronze in the 2019 AIBA Women's World Boxing Championships held in Russia. In 2020, Lovlina was honoured with the Arjuna Award and the Khel Ratna Award in 2021.

Lovlina Borgohain: The Boxing Champion

The next step was the Tokyo Olympics. Lovlina chopped off her waist-length hair as it hindered her boxing. Then she expanded on her jab, a punch executed with the hand near the face, typically below the opponent's chin.

Just like the muddy track in Baromukhia, Lovlina's path to success was not a smooth one. She faced multiple barriers and endured hardships to make it to the victory stand.

Events spiralled out of control as the country went under lockdown because of the pandemic. Lovlina visited her mother in Kolkata, who was scheduled for a kidney transplant. She tested positive for the virus a day before her scheduled departure for a training trip to Europe. It was a major setback, but she did not give up. Back in her village, she filled her time by working in the paddy fields and honing her skills, using water bottles and empty gas cylinders. In addition, she provided food packets to those who needed them.

> Following her victory over the reigning world champion at the Tokyo Olympics, Lovlina became the first Assamese to win an Olympic medal.

By the time Lovlina reached Tokyo for the Olympics, she had full confidence in her ability to win. The entire village of Baromukhia was glued to the television, watching her semi-final bout against the reigning world champion. They erupted in cheers as she stepped into the ring, powered by her favourite slogan. Fireworks and jubilation erupted as she triumphed over her opponent, securing the bronze medal in the Women's Welterweight category. Lovlina joined the ranks of Mary Kom and Vijender Singh as the third Indian boxer to win an Olympic medal. Such was the bout's importance that the Assam Assembly took a 30-minute break to watch her box in the Tokyo Olympics semi-finals.

A hero's welcome awaited Lovlina as she touched down at the Dimapur airport. She was escorted by the local MLA and senior police officers on her journey home. On the way she was greeted by a large number of people who had come to support and cheer for the athlete who became the first Assamese to win an Olympic medal. To the people, the bronze medal she won at the Tokyo Olympics held greater significance than a gold one.

The celebrations in Baromukhia started with a ceremony honouring her at her former school, Barpathar Higher Secondary School. First, a 50-kilogram cake was cut and then there was a dazzling display of fireworks in the sky. Lovlina's accomplishment as a 23-year-old was validated by the warm reception.

Lovlina not only won a medal but also earned people's love and respect. She brought a road, hospital and sports complex to her village, something the sons couldn't do. The Borgohains, with their two elder daughters in the Central Industrial Security Force and Border Security Force, respectively, and the youngest excelling as an athlete, proved the villagers wrong. They had proved that daughters could do as well as sons if nurtured with affection and attention.

From winning an Olympic medal, Lovlina went on to win gold in Asian Championships in 2022. Despite winning the bronze in 69 kg at Tokyo, she has switched to the 75 kg category for the 2024 Paris Olympics because of the 69 kg category being eliminated.

In 2022, Lovlina Borgohain was appointed as deputy superintendent of police and elected as chair and a voting member on the Board of Directors for the International Boxing Association (amateur) Athletes' Committee.

Lovlina Borgohain: The Boxing Champion

On 26 March 2023, Lovlina emerged victorious in the 75 kg category at the Women's World Boxing Championships, claiming the gold medal.

Lovlina faced disappointment at the 2023 Asian Games in Hangzhou. She was defeated in the final by China's Li Qian, a former World champion and two-time Olympic medallist. Lovlina bowed out with a silver medal in the 75 kg category. It was her first silver medal at a major event and it secured her place in the Paris Olympics.

She is now committed to winning a gold at the 2024 Paris Olympics.

Mary Kom: The Queen of Boxing

The Story

Born on 24 November 1982, Mary Kom comes from Kangathei, a village in Manipur. Her parents named her Mangte Chungneijang Mary Kom. In her language, the word *chungnei* means 'wealthy' and *jang* signifies 'agile'. Later, she shortened her name to M.C. Mary Kom for ease. Her parents, Mangte Tonpa Kom and Mangte Akham Kom, worked as farm labourers in the fields of the village chief and were very poor.

The family lived in a thatched bamboo hut plastered with mud and cow dung. The family grew larger when two more children were born to the couple. Mary's parents worked tirelessly to take care of their children. Besides working in the fields, her father hunted and fished too. He sold the catch to bring in more money. Her mother added to the family income by growing vegetables in the kitchen garden, weaving shawls and selling them in the market.

Being the oldest of the siblings, Mary had to look after them, do household chores and help her parents in the fields too. Since money was always tight, food was scarce for the family. Thus, Mary had to learn to hunt, fish and grow vegetables along with her parents.

Despite the difficulties, Mangte Tonpa Kom made sure Mary could attend Loktak Christian Model High School, which was an hour's walk from the village. Mary's enthusiasm for sports grew during her time in school, leading her to compete in javelin throw and 400-metre races. The decision to become a boxer came after watching Dingko Singh, a boxer from Manipur who won gold at the 1998 Asian Games, in action. At 15, Mary enrolled in a sports academy in Imphal and started training under a coach. Her parents did not know that she was training for boxing.

Mary knew her father would disapprove of boxing. Like most people in her village, he saw it as a man's game. She decided to keep it a secret. It wasn't until her name appeared in the newspaper after winning the 2000 state boxing championship that her father discovered she had taken up boxing. It was a difficult period for Mary. Making time for training because of her family responsibilities was a huge challenge. The lack of money made it impossible for her to afford equipment and training.

Mary's father became furious upon discovering her interest in boxing. Besides, he was also anxious about providing her with the diet necessary for a sportsperson.

Eventually, Mary's father decided to support his determined daughter unconditionally. Once she had got parental approval, Mary abandoned her studies and focused on boxing.

The Journey

When she was 18, Mary competed in her first international event. It was the AIBA Women's Boxing Championships in 2001. Her performance in the championship earned her the silver medal. She returned for the 2002 AIBA Women's Boxing Championships and won a gold medal. Thereafter, Mary created a world record by winning eight medals in the AIBA Women's Boxing Championships. She earned an impressive tally of six gold medals, one silver and one bronze. She now held the top position in the AIBA world rankings for the flyweight category.

In 2001, while en route to the training camp by train, Mary fell victim to a theft. She lost both her money and passport. Then, she met Karung Onler, a young man who was studying to be a lawyer. Onler was also the president of the North-East students' body in New Delhi. He helped Mary in every imaginable way and the two of them developed a deep affection for one another. They got married in 2005, after which Mary took a break from boxing in 2007 when she gave birth to twin boys. While she was overjoyed on becoming a mother, she needed to train herself well in order to return to the game with renewed strength and stamina.

Mary Kom made a triumphant comeback to boxing, earning a silver medal at the Asian Women's Boxing Championships in India. At the AIBA Women's World Boxing Championships in China in 2008, she secured her fourth consecutive gold medal. Her sparring skills were unharmed by the long break. A gritty fighter all her life, she has braved life's adversities and many opponents in the boxing ring. She is now considered the greatest female boxer because of her superlative performance. Mary proved that the harder you fight, the sweeter are the rewards in the end.

> Mary Kom created history by winning a bronze at the 2012 London Olympics, becoming the first Indian woman boxer to win an Olympic medal in the 51 kg category.

Mary Kom made history on 8 August 2012 by winning a bronze at the London Olympics and becoming the first Indian woman boxer to win an Olympic medal in the 51 kg category. Just like an unstoppable storm, she stormed through the competitions and collected multiple medals. In the 2014 Asian Games, she won a gold medal and continued her success by winning another gold in the 2015 Commonwealth Games. She made history as the first Indian woman to win gold in both the Asian and Commonwealth Games. At 38, the six-time world champion then shifted her focus to the 2020 Tokyo Olympic Games.

Mary's chances of winning a gold medal in the 2020 Tokyo Games were dashed when she crashed out by a single point. Unfortunately, it was her last chance at the Olympic Games.

The list of Mary Kom's awards and recognitions is long. She has received many awards, from the Arjuna Award to the Padma Bhushan, Padma Vibushan and Padma Shri. The AIBA gave her the nickname Magnificent Mary. So phenomenal is her journey that it found its way to the big screen too, along with an autobiography.

She is deeply passionate about animal rights and works with People for the Ethical Treatment of Animals (PETA).

Mary Kom has been honoured with numerous awards, including the Arjuna Award, the Padma Bhushan, the Padma Vibushan and the Padma Shri.

In order to give back to her people, she also founded the Mary Kom Regional Boxing Federation, which runs the Mary Kom Boxing Academy. In 2015, the academy was renamed Mary Kom–SAI Boxing Academy in Imphal, which mentors aspiring young talent and provides free training to underprivileged girls. Her dream is to produce a thousand Mary Koms.

Nikhat Zareen: The Punch Prodigy

The Story

Nikhat Zareen was born on 14 June 1996 in the Nizamabad district of Telangana. She is the third of four daughters born to Mohammad Jameel Ahmad and Parveen Sultana. Her father, who worked as a salesperson, is a sportsman at heart. An amateur cricketer and footballer in his youth, Jameel Ahmad dreamed that one of his daughters would take up sports someday. His other daughters were more academically driven and quieter than Nikhat, who was always getting into trouble. She was the naughtiest girl in Vishesh Vihar, where they lived.

During the summer vacations, Jameel Ahmad received complaints about Nikhat from his neighbours every day. She was either beating up their children or stealing mangoes and guavas from their trees.

One evening, he took his daughters to the ground, so they could play some game. One of them showed an interest in handball and another in basketball. It was then that Jameel Ahmad really noted the sporty built and attitude of his third daughter, Nikhat Zareen, who at that time dreamed of joining the Indian Police Services as an officer.

Once Jameel Ahmad spotted the potential in his daughter, he didn't let the grass grow under his feet. He bought a tracksuit for her and began training Nikhat for 100- and 200-metre races. The girl proved her father right by winning gold and becoming the district champion in both the sprinting events. One day, while training at the secretariat ground, which had multiple sporting activities, she noticed there were girls in all kinds of sports, but none in the boxing ring.

She asked her father why this was so. He replied that a lot of power and speed along with courage and strength were required to hit one's opponent in boxing. He added that people thought girls did not have the fight in them.

Her father's words set Nikhat thinking. She had never thought of girls being weaker or lesser than boys. Her uncle, Shamsuddin, was a boxing coach. His sons, Ehteshamuddin and Hussamuddin, were also boxers. Seeing them in action triggered Nikhat's interest in the sport and she decided to become a boxer. Jameel Ahmad supported her decision and started training his daughter. However, Nikhat's mother, Parveen, was against this decision.

> Nikhat's father, Jameel Ahmad, noticed his daughter's sporty build and attitude. He trained her and encouraged her to hone her skills.

The Journey

Deciding to become a boxer was easy, but making progress was difficult. Nikhat faced a lot of hurdles in her path to the boxing ring. Coming from a small town inhabited by conservative people caused Nikhat and her family to brave a lot of humiliating comments. They would often pass inappropriate remarks on Nikhat for wearing shorts and vests while training and said that Nikhat would never be able to get married—her face would be scarred from injuries sustained while playing. Such taunts hurt Nikhat's mother too, who was already not happy with her daughter's decision to be a boxer. However, Nikhat turned a deaf ear and put her heart into the one thing she knew best—to hone her skill and become a good boxer.

At the time, girls did not enter the boxing ring in Nizamabad, so Nikhat had to practise with boys. In her first sparring session with a boy, he hit her with all his strength, which resulted in Nikhat sustaining injuries—a black eye and scars all over. She returned home in a blood-stained t-shirt. Fearing her mother's reaction, Nikhat locked herself in the bathroom. Worried for her daughter, Parveen forced her to come out of the bathroom. She took one look at Nikhat's face and began crying. When Parveen lamented over the marriage prospects of their daughter, Nikhat's father reassured her that one day their daughter's brilliance would silence every naysayer. And Nikhat proved him right.

After training her for a year, Jameel Ahmad took Nikhat to the SAI camp. There she trained under I. Venkateswara Rao, a Dronacharya awardee. There was no looking back after that. The spunky girl won the sub-junior national title at 14 and her first international gold medal at the Youth World Championships held in Turkey. Next, she won a silver medal at the Youth World Championships held in Bulgaria. The same year, she won a gold medal at the International Boxing Championships in Serbia.

Not everything went smoothly for Nikhat thereafter. She suffered a painful shoulder dislocation that required surgery and extensive rehabilitation. It was a significant setback that led her to forgo training for a whole year, resulting in her absence from notable events like the World Championships, Commonwealth Games and Asian Games.

The injury gave her time to reflect on many matters, both physical and emotional.

Nikhat was determined to recover and return to the boxing ring. She was intent on making a name for herself in the world of sports. She made a remarkable comeback by winning a silver medal in the 2018 Belgrade Winner International Championship and followed it up first with a bronze in the 2019 Asian Championships and later a gold in the Strandja boxing tournament. By this time, winning national championships was an easy feat for the champion. The determined girl focused on the upcoming championships that would lead to the Olympics. Little did she know that her challenges were far from over.

Like most athletes and boxers, Nikhat was an ardent fan of Mary Kom, who had won a record of six golds at the World Championships and a bronze medal in the Olympics. Just like Mary Kom, Nikhat also competed in the flyweight category and it was widely known that only one of them would be chosen for the Olympics by the selection committee.

When the time for selection came around, the federation chose Mary Kom for the qualifying event. Not willing to yield, Nikhat Zareen wrote to Kiren Rijiju, requesting a bout between Mary Kom and herself. It brought her a lot of brickbats from the public and sports lovers. Mary Kom was everyone's favourite and by asking for a bout with her, Nikhat had unintentionally antagonized Mary's fans. The media wrote dozens of articles on the ugly spat between the two champions. Everyone waited eagerly for the bout because the winner would compete at the qualifying event leading to the 2020 Tokyo Olympics. Though Mary Kom won the bout and was selected to go for the qualifying event, it was Nikhat's courage for a fair chance that was commendable.

The defeat hurt Nikhat. But she tried to channel it well and become stronger, both physically and mentally. Driven by raging hunger, she worked harder than ever.

Nikhat went on a winning spree. She won the 2021 National Championship and followed it up with a bronze at the Bosphorus Open in the same year. In February 2022, she defeated Tetiana Kob of Ukraine and clinched a gold medal in the 73rd Strandja Memorial Boxing Tournament in Sofia, Bulgaria. This was her second gold in the prestigious Strandja boxing tournament.

On 19 May 2022, Nikhat was competing in the IBA Women's World Boxing Championships in Turkey. It was a chance to prove her mettle and she sparred as though there was no tomorrow. She trounced her opponent Jitpong Jutamas with an impressive score of 5-0, stunning the spectators. Minutes later, her name was called out and Nikhat roared and punched the air. Tears rolled down her cheeks. She had done it.

Nikhat Zareen thus became the world champion and became the fifth Indian woman to be so crowned. It had taken her 11 years, but she had finally achieved her dream. She had punched and fought for every victory along the way. Her rollercoaster journey was worth winning the World Championships medal. Accolades kept pouring in from all over. Right from the prime minister to sports legends and film stars, everyone congratulated the world champion.

On 26 March 2023, Nikhat continued her winning spree by clinching her second Women's World Championships title in the 50 kg

> After defeating Jitpong Jutamas in 2022 in the IBA Women's World Boxing Championships, Nikhat became the world champion.

category after defeating Vietnam's Nguyen Thi Tam. She confessed that she barely had any sleep the night before the bout. It was a tremendous effort for Nikhat. She had to win six bouts in 12 days to win the title. The champion, a firm believer in positive thinking, declared that she had manifested her two world titles and the Commonwealth Games title. She drew a gold medal with the word 'Champion' written on it and pasted it on her bed. Seeing it each day gave her the motivation to win the title, including a prize money of 100,000 US dollars and an SUV from the sponsors.

Setbacks are a part of an athlete's career. In the 2023 Asian Games at Hangzhou, Nikhat secured a bronze medal in the women's 50 kg boxing event after losing in the semi-final match. This served as an Olympic qualifier too. Nikhat is committed to bettering her game as she makes her Olympic debut at the 2024 Paris Olympics. She has also won a gold for India at the Eldora Cup 2024 in Kazakhstan.

Nikhat, a foodie, loves gorging on biryani, *tahari* and homecooked *khatti daal* — her mother's special.

Chess

1. Chess originated in India during the Gupta period about 1,500 years ago. It went by the name of Chaturanga.
2. The game was introduced to Europe in 1090. They played the game on a board that had light and dark squares, just like it does today. The game was given the name 'Chess'.
3. The winner uses the word 'Checkmate' when the opponent is unable to make any more moves. The word originated from the Persian phrase *Shah Mat*, which means the king is dead.
4. The game of chess is played on a square board comprising 64 smaller squares. Each player receives 16 pieces, including 8 pawns, 2 knights, 2 bishops, 2 rooks, 1 queen and 1 king.
5. The title of Chess Grandmaster (GM) is a coveted honour granted by the Fédération Internationale des Échecs (FIDE), or the International Chess Federation.
6. FIDE, founded in Paris in July 1924, is now based in Switzerland and is the governing body for all chess federations and conducts international competitions.
7. The Elo rating system was officially adopted by the US Chess Federation in 1960 and by FIDE in 1970.

8. Since 2015, the World Youth Chess Championships for boys and girls under the ages of 8, 10, 12, 14, 16 and 18 held every year have been split into 'World Cadets Chess Championships' for Under-8, Under-10 and Under-12, and 'World Youth Chess Championships' for categories Under-14, Under-16 and Under-18.

9. The record for the longest chess game was set in Belgrade in 1989. Nikolić and Arsović played a game that lasted 20 hours and 15 minutes.

10. The first game of chess in space took place in 1970 with two astronauts.

11. The record for the highest rating in history has been held by Magnus Carlsen since July 2011.

INTERNATIONAL CHESS MASTER at 10

Praggnanandhaa Rameshbabu

CHESS

Praggnanandhaa R.: The Grandmaster

The Story

Praggnanandhaa Rameshbabu, popularly known as Praggu, was born on 10 August 2005 in Padi, Chennai. Little did his parents know that their son would one day be a brilliant chess player. His father, Rameshbabu, works in the Tamil Nadu State Cooperative Bank and his mother, Nagalakshmi, is a homemaker. They named their son Praggnanandhaa as suggested by a temple priest.

It so happened that his sister, Vaishali, four years older than Praggu, was very fond of watching television as a child. Instead of studying or playing, she spent a lot of time watching cartoons. Her parents were worried that she was fast becoming a television addict. When she was 6 years old, in order to wean her off television they enrolled her in chess and drawing classes. Perhaps Rameshbabu and his wife were inspired by the popularity of the game in Chennai, the chess capital of India. The couple was pleasantly surprised when the girl took to chess like a fish to water. Their plan worked wonderfully and soon, Vaishali was quite addicted to chess. Thus, the stage was already set for Praggu to enter the world of chess, thanks to his sister.

As a toddler, Praggu saw his sister play chess and soon got interested in the game. She too indulged his interest by telling him about it. He was a keen learner and surprised his parents by playing chess even before he was 4. Rameshbabu and Nagalakshmi were delighted to see their children taking to chess. Interestingly, neither of them played chess themselves.

Soon, Praggu and his sister were playing chess regularly. They both loved the game and played against each other. It helped to sharpen their brain and kept them out of mischief. The cherry on the cake was that the regular habit of playing improved their game tremendously and the healthy competition between the siblings helped. They were constantly applying complex strategies to outdo each other, taking their game to a higher level.

Once Praggu had acquired remarkable skill in playing against his sister, he was ready to soar higher and test his game on the world stage.

The Journey

In December 2013, Praggu debuted internationally at the Youth World Chess Championship held at Al Ain, United Arab Emirates, and won the title of FIDE Master. He was just 7. The win boosted his confidence, causing him to aim even higher. His persistent effort led Praggu to win in the Under-10 boys category in 2015. He earned the title of International Master at 10—he was the youngest at the time to do so—and the GM at age 12, the second youngest at the time to do so.

His achievements drew the attention of the stalwarts of the game. Magnus Carlsen, the Norwegian GM and reigning five-time World Champion, had attained a rating of Elo 2882, the highest ever. A dream was taking shape in Praggu's mind—he wanted to reach Elo 3000 in the future and he began working towards it. The Elo rating system, created by Arpad Elo, measures relative strength of a player in games such as chess.

Praggu's parents put him in the Chess Gurukul Academy run by R.B. Ramesh, a GM himself. He and Aarthie Ramaswamy, a Woman Grandmaster (WGM), would train their pupils, helping them learn the intricacies of chess. Praggu and some boys would arrive there early so they could play 'hide and seek' before their chess training began.

With two chess-playing children, the cost of coaching, travelling and lodging when they played tournaments was becoming a challenge. But both Rameshbabu and Nagalakshmi spared no effort and continued to encourage the children. The struggle continued until 2015, when Praggu found sponsors and things brightened up. With the backing of their supportive parents, Praggu and his sister performed excellently and kept winning medals at the state, national and international levels.

Being a bank employee their father had to go to work, so it was the mother who accompanied the children whenever they had to go out of town to play chess tournaments. She ensured that her children got their comfort food. Since Praggu wasn't used to different cuisines, Nagalakshmi carried her rice cooker to wherever he travelled, so she could cook curd rice or rasam rice for him.

> Praggu was trained at the Chess Gurukul Academy by R.B. Ramesh and Aarthie Ramaswamy, both of whom were Grandmasters themselves.

Besides financial struggles, frequent power cuts and broadband connectivity posed a challenge for Praggu and his sister. To ensure that their practice sessions did not suffer during online tournaments, Rameshbabu installed an inverter and two separate broadband connections at home so that the two children could play online practice games and tournaments without any interruptions. This came in handy during the pandemic too, when everyone was confined indoors.

Chess is a quiet game, which requires much concentration on every move. As a chess player, one must be patient, as each move demands careful calculation and strategy. Sometimes the game can last for hours, which calls for mental as well as physical stamina. Thus, playing a sport like chess demands dedicating huge amounts of time. Since Praggu had been a chess prodigy, winning world titles from the age of 7, it interfered with his studies. Praggu attends the Velammal School, which is very supportive of its chess-playing students. The school is known for promoting chess and creating chess GMs, so it is flexible about attendance and examinations, which allows the students to concentrate on the game.

Praggu beat the Norwegian superstar Magnus Carlsen, the world number one in chess at the time, to achieve the biggest win of his career.

In 2017, Praggu clinched his first GM title by winning the World Junior Grandmaster Championship. One must bag three Grandmaster Norms (GN) to become a GM. The time finally arrived for Praggu in June 2018. At the Gredine Open Tournament at Urtijei in Italy, he bagged the third and final GN and became the second youngest person in chess history to become a GM.

Then, in 2022, Praggu achieved the biggest win of his career by beating Magnus Carlsen, the world number one in chess. He is only the third Indian after Viswanathan Anand and P. Harikrishna to beat the Norwegian superstar, the reigning world champion. It was an incredible achievement.

It is every chess player's dream to trounce the world champion and Praggu finally translated his dream into a win. It was a vindication of all the hard work when he got an applause and a thumbs-up even from his opponent, Carlsen.

When asked what he intended to do after his historic win, Praggu responded in his usual pragmatic manner that it was time to go to bed! It was 2.30 a.m.

The country was overjoyed to witness Praggu's grand victory. There were celebrations in Chennai. His friends and students at Velammal School along with a host of other people came to receive Praggu at the airport. He was garlanded, photographed and interviewed.

Sachin Tendulkar was one amongst a host of sporting legends to congratulate him. Praggu's idol, Vishwanathan Anand, invited him home to celebrate the victory. His victory hugely inspired young chess aspirants too.

As Praggu continued to hone his game, he faced the legendary Magnus Carlsen one more time at the Chess World Cup 2023 in Baku, Azerbaijan. It was a tough match. Praggu lost to Carlsen, but his second spot earned him a spot at the Candidates Tournament, making him the second Indian to do so. The 18-year-old prodigy made history in Indian chess. He became the second Indian after Viswanathan Anand to reach the Chess World Cup final.

On 18 January 2024, Praggu achieved a significant victory in the Tata Steel Chess Tournament by defeating Ding Liren, the world champion from China. This win also propelled him to surpass Viswanathan Anand as the top-rated Indian player.

R.B. Ramesh, Praggu's coach, mentor and motivator, claimed Praggu to be one of the most ambitious chess players of his generation—one who had started as early as 4.

Praggu's single-minded pursuit of the game has definitely paid rich dividends. Pitting his brain repeatedly against his sister from an early age offered a huge advantage to Praggu. He also pays critical attention to his physical health since playing chess involves sitting for long hours. Thus, Praggu cycles and plays table tennis whenever he finds the time. Playing cricket with his cousins and watching comedy movies also help him relax. Contrary to his serious demeanour while playing chess, Praggu is fun-loving, enjoys cracking jokes and likes to play the fool a lot.

The close relationship Praggu enjoys with his parents and sister is perhaps his panacea for the stress of a chess tournament against the best in the world. His self-confidence has also taken him where he deserves to be. Praggu's sister, Vaishali, joined the GM ranks in December 2023. The duo holds the distinction of being the world's first brother-sister GMs. The siblings breathe and talk the game. The shelves of the cabinet in their house are lined with numerous trophies that they have won.

Cricket

1. Cricket originated as a children's game in England during the 1600s. Charles Lennox, who was the second Duke of Richmond, and Alan Brodrick penned the first written rules for cricket in 1728. The Marylebone Cricket Club (MCC) drafted the first laws of the game in 1788.
2. The British army took on the English settlers in what was the first recorded cricket match in India in 1751.
3. The Calcutta Cricket Club was established in 1792. It is the second-oldest cricket club in the world, after the MCC.
4. The Parsis were the first Indian civilian community to play cricket. In 1848, they established the Oriental Cricket Club in Bombay (now Mumbai). The Young Zoroastrian Club was established in 1850.
5. The Hindu Gymkhana, Bombay was set up in 1866.
6. William Gilbert Grace is known as the father of cricket.
7. There are several variations of cricket, but the three major formats are Twenty20 (T20), One-Day Internationals (ODI) and Test matches. Among these, the Test match is the traditional form that has been played since 1877.

8. The biggest event in limited-overs cricket is the World Cup, which is organized by the International Cricket Council (ICC). The ICC was founded in 1909 as the Imperial Cricket Conference.

9. The ICC Women's Cricket World Cup is the oldest cricket world championship. The first tournament took place in 1973 and was hosted by England.

10. The first cricket ODI World Cup for men was held in 1975. It is now held every four years.

11. The weight of the cricket ball must lie between 155.9 and 163 grams. It is made with a cork core, and then wrapped in several yarn layers. The outer casing, crafted from leather, is coated with lacquer. The colour of a cricket ball can be red or white.

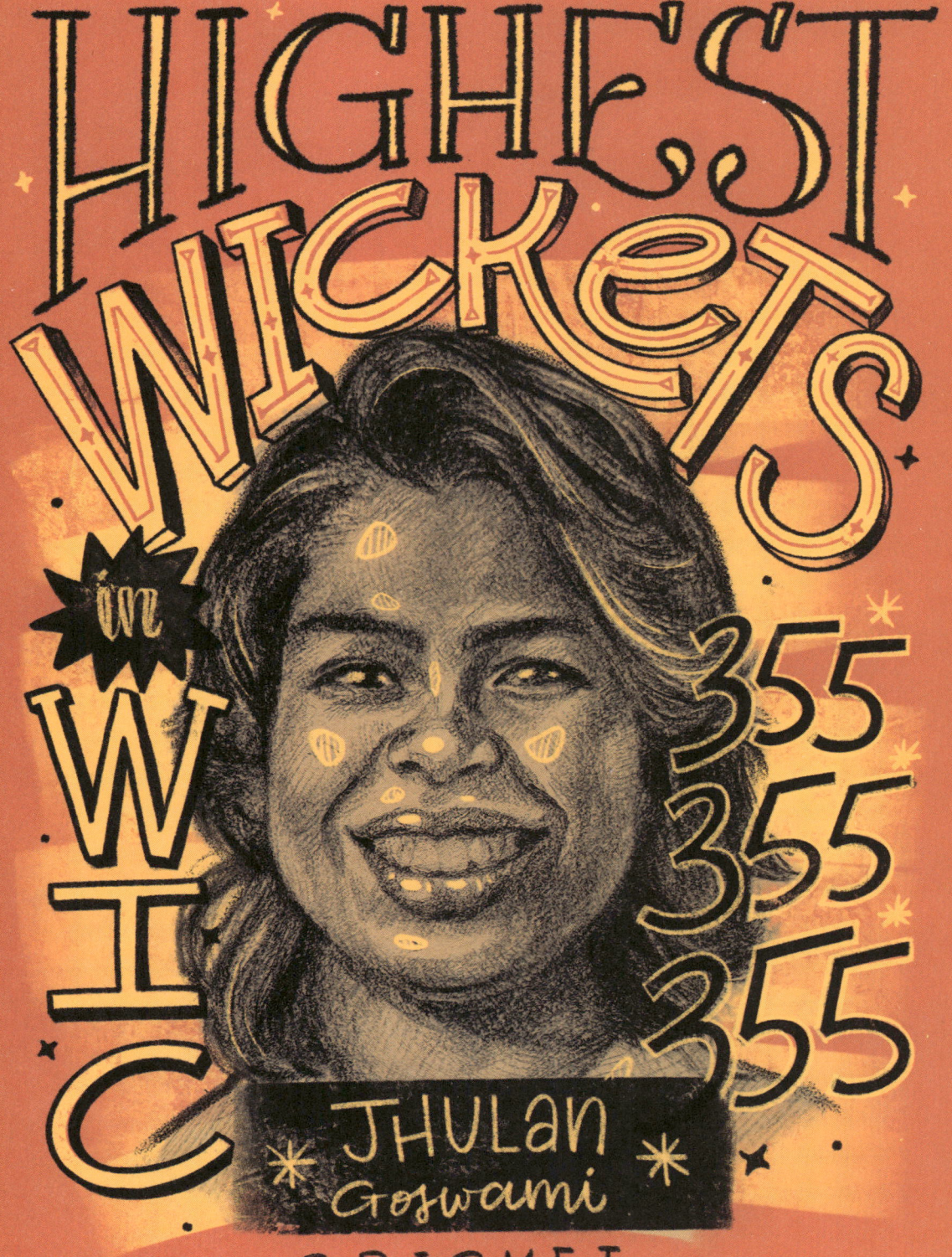

Jhulan Goswami: The Chakdaha Express

The Story

The one name cricket lovers have been hearing for the past few years is Jhulan Goswami. Like Mithali Raj, Jhulan's name has attained cult status in women's cricket. It all began on 25 November 1982 when Jhulan Goswami was born to a middle-class family in a small town named Chakdaha in West Bengal. Nishit and Jharna Goswami had no idea their daughter would one day become a famous cricketer and play for the country.

The child began displaying her love for sports at an early age. In her early years, Jhulan was interested in football—one of the most popular and loved sports in Bengal. Jhulan was so fond of the game that she would often watch it on television. One day, she accidentally switched to a different channel where the 1992 Cricket World Cup was playing. So fascinated was the girl that she quickly traded her love for football for an interest in cricket. She began playing cricket with a few boys in the neighbourhood. It shocked her conservative neighbours, who would often criticize her parents, but that didn't deter Jhulan from doing what she wanted to do. Nothing could change her mind about playing cricket.

The Journey

Her passion for the game caused her parents to rethink their view about a girl—their daughter—playing cricket. However, that was just the beginning of her arduous journey. Chakdaha being a small town lacked the infrastructure that she needed for training. The only way to follow her dream was to travel to Kolkata, which would take her a couple of hours by train. Doing so meant a significant loss of her school time. Giving up her studies was not an option, but Jhulan was equally against giving up cricket. She decided it was time to pursue both.

She would wake up at an early hour, board the first train to Kolkata to reach the training ground by 7.30 a.m. Once her training was over, she would board a return train to Chakdaha and go to school. She continued to do this thrice every week. Trying to keep up with both her training and studies exhausted her, but Jhulan was determined to get her way.

Jhulan was 15 when her life took an eventful turn. The 1997 Women's Cricket World Cup was scheduled to be played at the Eden Gardens in Kolkata. To Jhulan's delight, she was designated as a ball girl for the event. A ball girl retrieves the ball when it goes beyond the boundary line. It was a lifetime opportunity for the teenager. She had the chance to watch the game from close quarters. Jhulan was fascinated by the Australian captain Belinda Clark's dazzling performance. Though she witnessed

> Jhulan was only 15 years old when she was designated as a ball girl at the 1997 Women's Cricket World Cup at the Eden Gardens in Kolkata.

the Australian women's team lifting the World Cup, Jhulan's mind was made—she would play cricket and lead her team to victory one day.

Jhulan trained harder than ever and made it into the Bengal women's cricket team. She made her international ODI debut against England in Chennai in 2002. The same year, she made her Test debut and played against England in Lucknow.

Although chosen to play as a bowler, Jhulan stunned the spectators with her batting skill when she partnered with Mithali Raj to set a world record of 157 runs at Taunton, England in 2002. It was a tremendous accomplishment, and Jhulan came to be known as a fast bowler and a competent all-rounder.

Jhulan soon earned the reputation of being one of the deadliest bowlers in women's cricket. She was nicknamed the Chakdaha Express.

The Indian women's cricket team reached the final of the 2005 World Cup, but they lost the match. The defeat rankled her, but it gave Jhulan the chance to work on her weaknesses.

A self-proclaimed struggler with failure, she learned to channel her energy to change things for herself and the team. Her big chance to make up for the defeat arrived in 2006 when the Indian women's cricket team travelled to England for a Test series. Jhulan scored an impressive second half-century against England and ended up with 5 wickets in each inning. It helped India register their first-ever series victory against England in the longest format. Her stupendous performance ended with her being named the

> In 2006, Jhulan's stupendous performance helped India register its first-ever Test series victory against England. She was named the Player of the Series.

Player of the Series. She was also honoured with a special award at the Castrol Awards in Mumbai. In 2007, she won the ICC Women's Player of the Year award.

In 2008, after Mithali Raj stepped down, Jhulan took over as the captain of the Indian women's cricket team.

Jhulan was awarded the prestigious Arjuna Award in 2010, and the Padma Shri in 2012. In 2017, Jhulan ranked as the number one ICC Women's ODI bowler. In April 2018, the Indian government issued a postage stamp to acknowledge her contribution to women's cricket. After playing 68 T20s and picking up 56 wickets, she announced her retirement from T20 internationals in August 2018, as she wanted to focus on ODI cricket. She was nominated for the ICC Women's ODI Cricketer of the Decade award in November 2020

Jhulan has set several records in her cricketing career. She took her 40th wicket in the 2022 World Cup held in New Zealand, thus surpassing the Australian cricketer Lyn Fullston's record as the highest wicket-taker in the history of Women's World Cup. Jhulan became the world's fastest woman bowler after Cathryn Fitzpatrick. Her bowling speed of 120 kmph has knocked off many wickets. She announced her retirement from ODI cricket in September 2022.

Jhulan is now a bowling consultant for the Indian Women's Cricket team.

From a ball girl to captaincy, the Chakdaha Express has come a long way. And now, her life has inspired a biopic with Anushka Sharma playing the lead role.

Mithali Raj: The Cricket Lynchpin

The Story

Mithali Raj was born to Dorai Raj and Leela Raj on 3 December 1982 in Jodhpur, Rajasthan, where her father was posted. Dorai Raj was in the Indian Air Force, and Leela is a homemaker. As a child, Mithali had never been interested in playing cricket, which was considered a boys' game. Like many girls from Tamilian families, Mithali learned Bharat Natyam for eight years. Interestingly, it was her love for sleeping till late that got her into cricket.

The Journey

Dorai Raj, whose background as a defence employee made him a stickler for discipline, wondered how he could get his daughter to rise early in the morning. Then, he had a brilliant idea. The family lived in Secunderabad at the time. Dorai Raj's elder son was training in cricket and had to be taken to St John's Cricket Academy at 6 a.m. for practice. Mithali's father insisted that she accompany them every morning. So, while her brother played cricket, she sat on one side and completed her homework. When bored, she picked up a bat and played to pass her time. Although she was not a trained player, the girl had picked up the nuances of the game by watching the boys play.

It didn't take long for Jyothi Prasad, a former cricketer and coach at the academy, to notice her skill. He advised Dorai Raj to take the girl to Sampath Kumar, the head coach of Hyderabad's two age-group teams. Sampath realized that Mithali was an unpolished diamond and took the ten-year-old girl under his wing and thus began her journey into the world of cricket. Bharat Natyam took a back seat as her cricket training took priority. Sampath Kumar was a strict coach who made his pupils undergo rigorous training, beginning in the wee hours. Waking up so early wouldn't have been easy for the girl who loved sleeping till late. Thus, under Kumar's eagle eye, Mithali began improving her batting and bowling skills.

> Sampath Kumar, the head coach of Hyderabad's cricket teams, recognized Mithali's cricketing skill and took her under his wing.

Although Mithali had no interest in playing cricket in her early years, she began loving the game and gave it her all. However, her pursuit of cricket earned the disapproval of her conservative grandparents, who felt she was better off learning Bharat Natyam. The disapproval was echoed by other relatives too. Mithali's parents were not spared either.

Apart from the social censure, Mithali had to match the expectations of a stern coach. He made her practice batting in narrow corridors and was a hard taskmaster.

The little girl batted, bowled and fielded for hours on end, often practising till late in the evening, so she would get used to the low light too. The training was intense, with Sampath Kumar often tying one of her hands behind her back, so she would learn to catch the ball with one hand alone. On some days, Mithali returned home exhausted and in tears.

It was a tough time for Mithali, but her hard work paid rich dividends when at 13, Mithali was selected to play for Andhra Pradesh. There was no looking back from then on. She debuted in ODIs in 1999, scoring 114 runs against Ireland at Milton Keynes, England. At 19, she scored her first double-century in red-ball cricket and became the youngest cricketer to do so. She broke Karen Rolton's record of the world's highest individual test score, and then she surpassed her own record by scoring 214 runs in a match against England. Her phenomenal performance in the game earned her the captaincy of the Indian women's cricket team.

Recognition and awards followed soon after. In 2003, Mithali received the Arjuna Award. 2005 was an eventful year as Mithali, newly appointed captain of the Indian women's cricket team, led them to their first-ever World Cup final. The women in blue, who had been struggling to make a mark, finally found recognition when the Board of Control for Cricket in India (BCCI) took women's cricket under its wing in 2006.

At 22, Mithali led her team to a phenomenal victory in the Test series in England in 2006. Under her captaincy, the women in blue went on a winning spree by winning the Asia Cup the same year. Soon, Mithali became the first Indian woman cricketer to cross 5,000 runs in ODI. In May 2008, her team won their fourth successive Asia Cup title.

The women in blue had finally arrived, and the country sat up and took notice. Mithali was unstoppable. After the 2013 Women's World Cup, Mithali was named the number one cricketer. In 2015, she received the Padma Shri. She also received the Wisden Indian Cricketer of the Year in 2015, becoming the first female cricketer to win the award.

She was named the Vogue Sportsperson of the Year in 2017 and made it to the list of BBC 100 Women the same year.

After playing for over two decades, Mithali Raj announced her retirement from all forms of international cricket on 8 June 2022. Her record of runs and wins in her 23-year-long career remains unparalleled. She has played 12 Tests and 232 ODIs, scoring a record 7,805 runs in ODIs, making her the most prolific batter of all time. The number of runs beats the tally of her closest rival, Charlotte Edwards, the former captain of England. Mithali also holds the record for the maximum number of matches captained by a woman, having led the women in blue 155 times, winning 89 of them.

Mithali has rewritten the history of women's cricket in India and paved the path for other players to be seen and celebrated for their brilliance.

> Mithali Raj was the first female cricketer to win the Wisden Cricketer of the Year in 2015. She was also awarded the Padma Shri the same year.

Sachin Tendulkar: Master Blaster

The Story

Sachin was born on 24 April 1973 in Dadar, Mumbai. His father, Ramesh Tendulkar, was a Marathi writer, while his mother, Rajni, worked for an insurance company. Named after his father's favourite music director, Sachin Dev Burman, Sachin is the youngest of four siblings.

As a boy, Sachin was quite mischievous. He was interested in tennis in those days. He idolized the tennis star John McEnroe and wore headbands and sweatbands.

One day, his elder brother, Ajit, took him to Ramakant Achrekar's academy at Shivaji Park, Mumbai. The idea was to channel the mischievous boy's energy into the game of cricket. Sachin, who was 11 at the time, was instantly taken up with the idea. He displayed promise, and Ramakant took him under his wing. That was the beginning of Sachin's romance with the game. He practised for hours, his focus unwavering. It is said that Ramakant offered a coin to the bowlers if they could dismiss Sachin. The coin would go to Sachin if no one could dismiss him. To date, the master blaster considers the 13 coins he got from Ramakant as his most prized assets.

Sachin showed great potential even before he passed out of his school, Sharadashram Vidyamandir High School, which had a strong cricket team and many cricketers among its alumni.

It was then that Sachin joined the M.R.F. Pace Foundation in Chennai to hone his bowling skills. Though he was turned down by them, it was here that he met the legendary Australian cricketer Dennis Lillee, who at the time was the founder-director of the Foundation. It was Lillee who suggested that Sachin stick to batting instead. The suggestion became a turning point in Sachin's life. By 14, he had established himself as a skilled batter. In a school tournament in 1988, he scored 326 runs in a record-breaking partnership with Vinod Kambli, where the duo notched 664 runs—the highest partnership score in cricket at the time. With this feat, Sachin attained fame as a child prodigy in his school and beyond.

Sachin made his ODI debut in the year 1989 against Pakistan. He was handed his maiden Test cap in November the same year.

The Journey

On 14 November 1987, Sachin was selected to play in the Ranji Trophy, but he remained a substitute player. His chance to play his first Ranji Trophy match came in December 1988. This time, he was determined to make his mark. He scored an unbeaten 100, which propelled him into the national team. He was now on a roll.

The very next year, in December 1989, Sachin made his ODI debut against Pakistan. The teenager had been handed his maiden Test cap in November and played his first international Test match against Pakistan the following month. He became the youngest Indian to play international Test cricket at the age of 16 years and 205 days.

It was a challenge for teenaged Sachin to play against Pakistan. Pakistani bowlers were among the best in the world, and Sachin had to face their ferocious bouncers. On 13 December 1989, during the fourth day of the fourth Test in Sialkot, a bouncer from Waqar Younis hit Sachin's nose, injuring him. Medics rushed to the ground as the youngster fell, writhing in pain. Everyone thought he would leave the crease, but Sachin refused all aid. Navjot Sidhu, who was Sachin's co-batter, also advised him to leave the crease, but Sachin said, '*Main khelega*', meaning 'I will play'. He wiped his nose and resumed batting. He scored 57 runs off 135 balls. His courage and ability to be unfazed in the midst of a tough ball elicited praise from the Pakistani team and cricket enthusiasts all over the world. If anything, that incident strengthened his resolve to up the ante.

Sachin's early years in international cricket were full of struggle as he learned to deal with pressures, pain and failures. But every experience is a learning one and he reacted to them with grit and determination. In 1992, a 19-year-old Sachin was invited by the Yorkshire County Cricket Club to play for their team. With that, he became the first overseas player to be selected to play for them. By the time he was 20, he had etched a remarkable record of having played 25 Tests, with a total of over 1,500 runs at 44, with five splendid centuries against three giants of the game—England and Australia (twice each), and South Africa.

In 1990, while returning from England with the Indian cricket team, Sachin's eyes met Anjali Mehta's, who had come to receive her

Sachin Tendulkar: Master Blaster

mother at the airport. It was a case of love at first sight. Thereafter, Sachin dated Anjali, who had studied medicine from the Grant Medical College, Mumbai and started working at Mumbai's Sir Jamsetjee Jejeebhoy Group of Hospitals. The two of them got engaged in 1994 and married on 24 May 1995.

Sachin's tour of Australia in 1992, where he scored two centuries, is considered one of his best. Sir Donald Bradman, one of the greatest batters, felt Sachin's technique was the same as his, and that was a big compliment for the Indian batting wizard.

The master blaster was awarded the Arjuna Award in 1994.

In the 1996 World Cup, the Indian team led by Mohammad Azharuddin reached the semi-finals. Sachin put up a fine show and scored 65 runs against Sri Lanka. He was named the captain of the Indian cricket team in 1996. At 23, he took over the reins from Azharuddin.

Sachin was awarded the Rajiv Gandhi Khel Ratna Award in 1998 and the Padma Shri in 1999. While Sachin continued to perform exceptionally well, his career was sometimes marred by brickbats too.

The toughest time was when the Indian cricket team was disqualified in the group stage of the 2007 World Cup. Sachin and other seasoned players were heckled as passions ran high.

Regardless, Sachin's long cricketing career is chequered with many firsts—both nationally and internationally. In December 2005, he scored his 35th century while playing a Test match against Sri Lanka, breaking Sunil Gavaskar's record. In June 2007, Tendulkar

> Sachin was awarded the Arjuna Award in 1994, the Rajiv Gandhi Khel Ratna Award in 1998 and the Padma Shri in 1999.

reached another major milestone when he became the first player to record 15,000 runs in ODI play.

He received the Padma Vibhushan in 2008. In 2010, he was named the ICC Cricketer of the Year.

In 2010, Sachin figured in the TIME100 list of Most Influential People in the World. The year 2011 was extremely special for Sachin as it was his last World Cup—one where the Indian cricket team created history, defeating Sri Lanka by six wickets. It was a World Cup that India won after 28 years.

The win had a special meaning for Sachin, who was able to fulfil his childhood dream. In November 2011, he became the first batter ever to score 15,000 runs in Test cricket. The very next month, he scored a double century against South Africa, which was the first double century ever scored in ODI cricket.

Sachin played for Mumbai Indians in the Indian Premier League (IPL) for five years, from 2008 to 2013. In November 2013 he was named the first UNICEF Regional Goodwill Ambassador for South Asia.

After a splendid cricketing career spanning nearly three decades, Sachin announced his retirement on 23 December 2012 from ODI cricket. He also retired from T20 Internationals but continued playing Test cricket until 2013. His last test match was at the famous Wankhede Stadium in Mumbai against West Indies in November 2013.

In April 2012, Sachin was nominated by the President of India as a member of the Rajya Sabha. He became the first active sportsperson to be a Member of Parliament (MP). He donated his salary for the complete term as MP to the Prime Minister's Relief Fund. He was also the first sportsperson to be awarded the Bharat Ratna, India's highest civilian honour, in 2013. The same year, he was listed at number 51 in the Forbes list of the World's Highest-Paid Athletes.

Sachin is actively involved in philanthropic activities. He sponsors underprivileged children through the NGO Apnalaya. Sachin's autobiography, *Playing It My Way*, broke all records to become an instant bestseller. Thereafter, many books have been written about his life.

As Andy Flower, Zimbabwean cricketer and coach, once said: 'There are two kinds of batsmen in the world. One, Sachin Tendulkar. Two, all the others.'

Smriti Mandhana: The Queen of Offside

The Story

Smriti was born on 18 July 1996 to Smita and Srinivas Mandhana. Her father is a chemical distributor in a textile company in Mumbai and mother is a homemaker. Smriti has a sibling, who is four years older.

When Smriti was 2, her father took a job in a private bank and the family moved to Madhavnagar in the Sangli district of Maharashtra. Srinivas, who had played cricket at district level, was keen for his son to excel in the game. Encouraged and inspired by his father, Smriti's brother, Shravan, took to cricket and reached the district level. As a result, while growing up, Smriti constantly heard her father and brother talking about cricket and its intricacies. It was inevitable that the little girl would start playing cricket and she did so at age 6.

The Journey

Smriti began by playing gully cricket with the neighbourhood boys. She could bat for a long time without getting out. At the age of 9, Smriti would play cricket with her brother and older boys. No one really taught her how to play—she learned by watching her brother play. Since her brother was left-handed, she too followed his style of batting and became left-handed.

Soon, Shravan started playing for the Maharashtra Under-16 team. Smriti insisted on accompanying her father to watch Shravan play. Srinivas was delighted to find her taking an interest in cricket and helped her practice. At first, he lobbed the ball gently at her, which irked the girl, who wanted to play serious cricket. At her insistence, he hurled the ball faster and was surprised to see her deftly handling it.

Smriti got picked up to play for the Maharashtra Under-15 cricket team at the age of 9. It was then that her family rallied behind her seriously. Her father started to look after her cricketing schedule, her mother took care of her diet and clothes, while her brother gave her practice at the nets. Playing for the Under-15 team boosted her confidence.

As she grew in stature, Smriti required more time and attention for practice. Unfortunately, neither her father nor her brother could spare much time. It would have been ideal if she could travel to Bengaluru or Mumbai to gain experience by playing with seasoned players. But she was too young to travel alone.

Smriti was selected to play for the Maharashtra Under-15 cricket team at the young age of 9 — an experience that boosted her confidence.

It was then that the junior state cricket coach Anant Tambwekar came to her rescue. A cricket pitch was prepared and she began her training under his strict watch. For all young sportspersons, balancing studies and sport is a tricky thing. Smriti had her share of challenges too. It was a hectic schedule, as she went for training in the morning, then to school and then again for practice at the nets in the evening.

Since there were not many girls playing cricket in Sangli, Smriti would practise with boys—sometimes she would be the only girl among 200–300 boys. Shravan was the most consistent partner during her practice.

It was a joyous moment for the family when Smriti was picked to play for the Maharashtra Under-19 team at 11. Soon she was playing with senior players, facing some of the most seasoned players. In her first match against Saurashtra, she scored 155 runs in style and impressed the spectators.

In 2011, 15-year-old Smriti was in a dilemma. While her cricketing career was going strong, the approaching board exams were weighing heavily on her mind. She was quite unsure about picking a stream for herself. Her mother's support and guidance helped her pick commerce.

Smriti stepped into international cricket in 2013. She played her first T20 match against Bangladesh during their tour of India. She was the highest scorer with 39 runs in 36 balls. India won the match by 10 runs. Five days later, she played her first ODI against the visiting Bangladesh team on 10 April 2013. Again, India won the match by 46 runs—Smriti scored an impressive 25 off 35 balls.

Meanwhile, she continued to play closer home for the Under-19 Maharashtra team against Gujarat, where she scored an unbeaten 224 off 150 balls in October 2013 in Vadodara and became the first Indian woman to score a double century in an ODI match. It was a major achievement that helped her clinch a spot in the Indian senior team.

In August 2014, Smriti made her test debut against England at the age of 18 years and 29 days. In both innings she was the second-highest scorer from the Indian side, scoring 22 and 51 runs. India won the Test by 6 wickets. It was a historic win for this was the Test after a gap of eight years and eight new Indian players had made their Test debut.

Smriti credits her success to the special bat gifted by her brother. Shravan, when playing for the Under-19 team, had met Rahul Dravid and told him about his sister's skill, requesting a cricket bat. Dravid took his practice bat, signed and gifted it to him, which Shravan presented to Smriti.

Dravid's bat became Smriti's talisman. Over the next few years, she played many memorable matches with it. Those who saw her play with Dravid's practice bat thought it was a bit too big for her and wondered why she had been using it. But Smriti liked the bat and executed many masterstrokes with it, including a double century.

In the second ODI during the Indian tour of Australia in February 2016, Smriti scored her first international century with a wonderful knock of 102 from 109 balls in Hobart. During the 2016 Women's Challenger Trophy, she played for India Red against India Blue in the finals at Vadodara. Her score of 62 off 82 balls helped her side win. She notched up 192 runs, becoming the top scorer in the tournament. She was the only Indian player to be named in the ICC Women's Team of the Year 2016.

The same year she signed up with Brisbane Heat to play in the Women's Big Bash League (WBBL). It was while playing in the WBBL in January 2017 that she was badly hurt. Her anterior cruciate ligament (ACL) injury was acute. She had to undergo surgery and rehabilitation, which put her participation in the upcoming 2017 Women's World Cup in doubt.

However, Smriti was declared fit to play in the 2017 World Cup and her knocks helped India make it to the finals. Unfortunately, in the finals on 23 July, India lost to England at Lord's. It was the second

Smriti Mandhana: The Queen of Offside

time Smriti was playing on the prestigious cricket ground and had failed to make an impact. Back in 2014, she had had her first chance to play at the Lord's but rains had played the spoilsport.

Smriti continued to prove herself to be powerful with the bat during the T20 World Cup 2018. In March 2018, she scored the fastest 50 against Australia in the women's Tri-Nation Series, taking just 30 balls to reach a half-century. In 2018, she was declared the ICC Women's Cricketer of the Year and the ICC Women's ODI Player of the Year.

In 2019, Smriti was the top-ranked batter by ICC, and Forbes put her in the Top 30 in the Under-30 category for her outstanding performance. The Government of India gave her the prestigious Arjuna Award. The same year, she was made the captain of the T20 team when Harmanpreet Kaur was injured in the very first match of the three-match series against England. Smriti became the youngest woman to captain the T20 team.

In 2019, Smriti Mandhana became the youngest woman to captain the Indian T20 team. She was also the top-ranked batter by ICC the same year.

Post COVID, though Smriti was in form, India failed to make it to the semi-finals in the Women's Cricket 2021–22 World Cup in New Zealand. Smriti was India's top scorer in the competition with 327 runs. She was awarded the ICC Women's Cricketer of the Year for the second time, becoming the second player in history to win the award twice.

The women's cricket team participated in the 2022 Commonwealth Games (CWG) at Birmingham. India entered the finals by beating England by 4 runs, but lost to Australia in the finals by 9 runs. In the match with Pakistan at the CWG, the Indian women defeated Pakistan by 8 wickets at Edgbaston, Birmingham. Smriti hit a magnificent unbeaten 63 off 42 balls.

The last series that the Indian captain Jhulan Goswami played was the ODI Series in September 2022 against England. In the third and final match, Jhulan could not score a single run but took 3 wickets for 30 runs. Smriti scored 50 off 79 balls. India won the match by 16 runs and the series by 3-0. It was a fitting farewell to Jhulan Goswami.

Smriti's crowning glory came after she led her team to win the gold medal in the 2022 Asian Games in Hangzhou in September 2023. It was the first-ever gold medal for the Indian women's cricket team. It was an emotional moment for Smriti as well as for the nation. In March 2024, Smriti led her IPL team, the Royal Challengers Bangalore, to a victory in the final against the Delhi Capitals.

Smriti is the third quickest Indian to score 1,000 runs in the T20 International format. She was also the 10th fastest batter in women's cricket history to achieve this feat. She took just 49 innings to break the 1,000-run mark.

Smriti enjoys spending time with the family. She loves *aloo parathas* made by her mother and misses them the most during her tours. Smriti is known for her calm demeanour during some of the most challenging games. She practices a 10-minute guided meditation before leaving for the stadium.

Football

1. Cuju, meaning kick-ball, was the name given to football when it was first invented in ancient China over 2,000 years ago. This makes football one of the world's oldest sports. It started as a military sport to train the troops. Cuju was played with a ball made from an animal bladder.

2. Fédération Internationale de Football Association (FIFA), which is the world governing body of association football, was founded in Paris in 1904. It has more member countries in it than the United Nations.

3. Stadium 974 in Qatar gets its name from the country's dialling code. It is constructed using shipping containers. This innovative football venue has a capacity of 40,000 and it can be completely dismantled. Stadium 974 hosted several matches during the World Cup 2022.

4. A Dutch football team called Nooit opgeven altijd doorzetten, Aangenaam door vermaak en nuttig door ontspanning, Combinatie Breda holds the record for the world's longest name. People commonly use the name NAC Breda when referring to them.

5. Sialkot in Pakistan manufactures over 80 per cent of the footballs that are used around the world. They have made the FIFA World Cup balls since 1982.
6. The duration of a football game is usually 90 minutes, with a 15-minute intermission after the first half. It is a tough game to play. The average distance run by a professional football player in one game is around 11.2 kilometres.
7. In 1958, the famous football player, Pele, won the World Cup at 17.

1st Indian to Play with SEVEN Football Clubs

BHAICHUNG Bhutia

FOOTBALL

Bhaichung Bhutia: The Sikkimese Sniper

The Story

Bhaichung Bhutia, who dominated the football scene in the 1990s and early 2000s, is the torchbearer and superstar of Indian football. He has been called 'God's gift to Indian football' by the football veteran I.M. Vijayan.

Bhaichung was born to a farmer's family in a remote and picturesque village called Tinkitam in Sikkim on 15 December 1976. He was called Ugen Sangey and nicknamed Bhaichung ('Little Brother' in Sikkimese). It became his proper name because when asked his name during school admission, he replied, 'Bhaichung'!

Bhaichung was a playful and bright child who showed tremendous interest in sports. Although he began his schooling at St Xavier's School in Pakyong, East Sikkim, at the age of 9 he moved to the Tashi Namgyal Academy in Gangtok after winning a football scholarship from the SAI. At Tashi Namgyal Academy, he proved to be a strong contender for prizes in various sports. He represented his school in athletics, basketball and badminton, besides football. A Maradona fan, Bhaichung practised early in the morning on wet and muddy grounds in his school days because he wanted to play like him. He made up for the lack of facilities in his village with determination and hard work.

After he lost his father, Dorji Dorma, quite early in life, Bhaichung's uncle, Karma Bhutia, took an active interest in his little nephew. Karma Bhutia, who was the manager of the Boys Football Club in Gangtok, spotted the potential in Bhaichung and guided him to take up football professionally.

Bhaichung's big break came after his superlative performance in the Subroto Cup 1992, where he was named the best player. His game drew the attention of Bhaskar Ganguly, the former goalkeeper of East Bengal Football Club. Ganguly asked him to consider joining the club and moving to Kolkata. In 1993, Bhaichung signed with the East Bengal Football Club in Kolkata and went on to become their highest scorer. He became a professional football player at 16. This was the beginning of a successful journey that spanned about 18 years.

> Bhaichung Bhutia joined the East Bengal Football Club in Kolkata in 1993 and went on to become its highest scorer. This was the beginning of a successful journey spanning nearly 18 years.

The Journey

In 1995, Bhaichung moved to Phagwara to play for JCT Mills, won the Indian National Football League and was named the 'Player of the Year'. He made his international debut against Thailand for the Nehru Cup in March 1995. In the tournament, he scored his debut international goal against Uzbekistan at 19, making him India's youngest-ever goal-scorer.

In 1997, Bhaichung returned to the East Bengal Football Club and created history by becoming the first player to score a hat-trick in a derby against the Mohun Bagan Athletic Club. He soon added another feather to his cap by becoming the youngest club captain at 21.

He was honoured with the Arjuna Award in 1998. In a series of firsts, he set a record by signing a three-year deal with Bury Football Club in 1999. Thus, Bhaichung became the first Indian to sign a contract with an English club.

On his return from England, he joined the Mohun Bagan Athletic Club in 2002, only to switch to the East Bengal Football Club in 2003. Bhaichung continued to represent the two clubs and the country in various matches and won many national and international championships. Under his leadership, the Indian team won the South Asian Football Federation (SAFF) Cup three times, the Nehru Cup twice, the LG Cup in 2002 and the Asian Football Challenge (AFC) Cup in 2008. He was named the Player of the Tournament in 2009 while playing the Nehru International Tournament.

> In 2011, Bhaichung Bhutia played his last football match at the Nehru Stadium against FC Bayern Munich, one of the biggest football clubs.

In 2008, Bhaichung was awarded the Padma Shri. In a detour from playing football, he took to the dance floor in May 2009 and became the winner of the dance reality show *Jhalak Dikhla Jaa* on Sony television.

In 2011, Bhaichung suffered an injury during an AFC Cup match and on 24 August 2011 he announced his retirement. At the time of retiring, he held the record of being the only Indian football player to have played in over 100 matches for the country, having scored 40 goals in 104 appearances. He is the first Indian football player to have played in seven football clubs. Besides playing with the top football clubs Mohun Bagan and East Bengal in West Bengal, he has also played for Jagatjit Cotton and Textile (JCT) FC, Bury FC, United Sikkim and two Malaysian clubs—Perak FA and Selangor MK Land.

In a packed Nehru Stadium, Bhaichung played his farewell match against FC Bayern Munich, which is one of the biggest clubs in football. India lost the match, but the spectators gave Bhaichung a standing ovation to acknowledge his contribution to Indian football.

Even after his retirement, Bhaichung continues to be committed to the cause of football. He has established the Bhaichung Bhutia Soccer Schools to train budding footballers. In 2014 he contested elections on behalf of Trinamool Congress in West Bengal and in 2018, he founded a political party called Hamro Sikkim Party. The year 2021 marked a significant milestone for Bhaichung Bhutia, who became the first Indian footballer to have a stadium named after him. The Bhaichung Bhutia Stadium in Namchi, South Sikkim, was inaugurated by the Sikkim Governor.

From the small village of Tinkitam to stardom, it has been a long journey for the Sikkim Striker. His message to budding football players is simple—just enjoy the game when playing and do not worry about performance.

Sunil Chhetri: Captain Fantastic

The Story

Sunil Chhetri was born in Secunderabad in Telangana on 3 August 1984. His father, Kharga Bahadur Chhetri, was in the army and served as an officer in the Corps of Electronic and Mechanical Engineers. As a child, Sunil Chhetri travelled all over the country wherever his father was posted. Like all army kids, he had to switch schools each time his father was transferred to a new place. As a result, he attended schools in Gangtok, Darjeeling, Kolkata and Delhi, and graduated from Asutosh College, Kolkata.

Sunil inherited his love for soccer from his parents. His father played for the army soccer team and his mother, Sushila, had played football for the Nepal national football team along with her twin sister. Sunil started playing when he was 4 or 5 years old, impressing his father with his deft handling of the ball even at that age.

There were many struggles on Sunil's road to success. Football was never a career option, as far as his father was concerned. For him education came first and then football. But, for the football fanatic, it was too strict an order. Sometimes, Sunil had to fight his way and even go against the wishes of his parents.

At 15, Sunil switched from Army Public School in Delhi to Mamta Modern School, without his father's knowledge because they gave a lot of importance to football. He also moved into the school's hostel so he could focus on the game. When his father came to know about it, he was furious. Many days later, only after watching him play at a practice session did he forgive him.

Sunil topped his school in class 11, but football continued to be central to his life. While still at school, Sunil played local matches—his team beat the local army team and also the Border Security Force football team. This boosted his morale, and he realized that playing football is what he wanted to do all his life.

The Journey

Sunil had just passed class 12 and was preparing for his college admission when he received an offer from Mohun Bagan Athletic Club. They wanted him to play for their club and signed him up for their upcoming domestic season in 2002. He was just 17.

During his three years with Mohun Bagan, he was under the mentorship of 1989 Arjuna awardee Subroto Bhattacharya, the former player of the Indian team who spent 17 years playing for Mohun Bagan. Soon, Sunil established himself as a useful member of the team and represented India in several international tournaments and helped India beat Pakistan in the 2004 SAFF Games and Cambodia in the 2007 Nehru Cup.

After his three-year stint with Mohun Bagan, which ended in 2005, Sunil switched to JCT FC. There, he

> Sunil received an offer from Mohun Bagan Athletic Club when he was just 17 years old and preparing for college. He signed up for their domestic season in 2002.

showed tremendous form and scored many goals, lifting the ranking of JCT FC. In the season 2006–07, he scored 11 goals and JCT FC finished second that year.

The East Bengal Football Club was impressed with Sunil's game and signed him for the season beginning in 2008. He had a wonderful inning with East Bengal and then in 2009 with Dempo Sports Club, Goa. In 2010 Sunil got an opportunity to play for Kansas City Wizards (now known as Sporting Kansas City) in the USA. With that, he became the third Indian after Mohammad Salim and Bhaichung Bhutia to play for an international club. He had another stint at Sporting Clube de Portugal (Sporting CP). After his return to India, Sunil Chhetri was named the captain of the Indian football team for the 2012 AFC Cup.

He also captained the Indian football team for the Nehru Cup tournament in the same year. Sunil has played for various other soccer clubs, namely Chirag United, Churchill Brothers, Bengaluru and Mumbai City FC. He recorded the maximum number of appearances of an Indian footballer and became the first Indian to play for three different countries.

Sunil was instrumental in India winning the Nehru Cup in 2007, 2009 and 2012 and the SAFF Championships in 2011, 2015, 2021 and 2023. He was named 'Player of the Year' by the All India Football Federation (AIFF) seven times. Undeniably, he is one of the best Indian football players. In 2011, he was awarded the Arjuna Award.

Sunil entered the Indian Super League (ISL) in 2015 and gave it a wonderful boost. His first outing was with the Mumbai City FC, but after two years he switched to Bengaluru FC. He scored many goals as a striker, which gave him the reputation of being a goal scoring machine. He became the first Indian to score a hat-trick in the ISL, helping Mumbai City FC win.

Sunil has scored the highest number of international goals by an Indian, the highest number of goals in the I-League and in ISL.

In the 2018 Intercontinental Cup in Mumbai on 1 June, India played against Chinese Taipei, winning with 5-0, including the Indian captain's hat-trick. It was a brilliant match, but Sunil Chhetri, the Indian captain, was very disappointed for the stands were almost empty. He took to social media and posted a video on Twitter with an appeal to all fellow Indians to come and watch the Indian national team play.

The video of his humble and earnest appeal went viral and the result was astounding. In the very next game on 4 June, in which India was up against Kenya in Mumbai, Mumbaikars turned out in hordes and the stadium was packed. Buoyed by the support, the Indian team put their best foot forward and beat Kenya 3-0, making it to the finals. In the final, India faced Kenya again and won by 2-0, both goals scored by Sunil.

> Sunil became the first Indian to play for three different countries. He has scored the highest number of international goals by an Indian.

Sunil is ranked the third-highest goal scorer in the world. In 2018, he surpassed Lionel Messi's record of 64 international goals. In 2019, he was awarded the Padma Shri, the fourth-highest civilian award in India. And in 2021 he got the Major Dhyan Chand Khel Ratna Award, the highest award in sports. He was the first Indian footballer to get the award.

The world football governing body, FIFA, has released a video series on the life and career of Sunil Chhetri, called *Captain Fantastic*, in recognition of his achievements and goal-scoring exploits. He is married to his long-time friend Sonam, who is the daughter of his coach at Mohun Bagan, Subroto Bhattacharya.

Sunil's message for young parents is to indulge with their kids at all levels to spot their natural talent. And if it happens to be in sports, they should encourage their children to take it up.

Sunil is ranked 3rd among active footballers in terms of international goals scored, with only Lionel Messi and Cristiano Ronaldo ahead of him. After playing for the country for 19 years, Sunil announced his retirement on 16 May 2024. The world will witness his excellence one last time at the FIFA World Cup qualifier against Kuwait on 6 June 2024.

Gymnastics

1. The word 'gymnastics' originates from the Greek words *gymnos* or *gymnazo*, which means 'to train or to exercise naked'.
2. The world's governing body for gymnastics is the International Gymnastics Federation (FIG). Since 1881, it holds the distinction of being the oldest international federation of an Olympic sport. It is headquartered in Lausanne, Switzerland, known as the Olympic Capital.
3. The 1984 Olympic Games in Los Angeles saw the introduction of rhythmic gymnastics as an independent discipline. The 1996 Olympic Games in Atlanta introduced the group event to the programme.
4. Germany's Friedrich Ludwig Jahn is acknowledged as the founder of modern gymnastics. During the 1800s, he invented the high bar, parallel bars, side bars, rings and balance beams. This equipment has now become an essential requirement in gymnastics.
5. The first gymnastics competition in the history of Olympic Games took place in Athens, Greece in 1896. Only in the 1928 Olympic Games did women's gymnastics become a part of the programme.
6. George Eyser, an American gymnast, made history by winning the Olympics in 1904 with a wooden leg.

Dipa Karmakar: The Produnova Girl

The Story

Dipa was born on 9 August 1993 in Agartala, Tripura. She is the second daughter of Dulal and Gauri Karmakar. Her father is a weightlifting coach in Agartala.

As a child, Dipa had an abundance of energy. She climbed trees, jumped and sprinted. Being a sportsperson, her father realized early that her energy could be put to good use. When she was just a little over 5, he enrolled the young girl in training with Soma Nandi, a national-level gymnast, as he wished for her to become a gymnast.

Dipa began training at the Vivekananda Byamagar under Soma's guidance. At this point she moved to a Bangla medium school as it was not very strict with attendance, unlike the English medium school that she had attended with her sister. This way she could have enough time to practise gymnastics. Her parents were unhappy with her decision but had to give in as she had made up her mind.

In the end, Dipa's choice turned out to be right. She won a gold medal at the Northeastern Games when she was only 9 years old. She competed in a borrowed costume and was barefoot because she did not own a pair of gymnastic shoes. The gold medal was her first.

The Journey

Dipa's second coach was Bisheshwar Nandi, a five-time national gymnast and six-time captain of the Indian gymnastics team. Much to his dismay, he realized that Dipa had flat feet, a condition where one or both feet have little to no arc. This poses a challenge for a gymnast as it can affect their take-off. Nandi conducted research on exercises that could shape and strengthen Dipa's arch. They consistently worked together to overcome the drawbacks. It took a lot of practice and exercise, but the results finally showed. Over time, the arches in Dipa's feet developed to a satisfactory level.

However, there were other challenges for Dipa. Her gymnasium was a shabby structure with a tin roof that leaked in the monsoon. Due to excessive rainfall in Tripura, the floor was wet most of the time. The gymnasts leaped over ingenious equipment fashioned out of discarded motor parts. They touched down on platforms composed of lumpy mattresses. The absence of proper training facilities in Agartala was a major setback for gymnasts.

There was hardly any space inside for floor training, so the gymnasts floor-trained on padded mats that were carried outside and spread. This could not be done during heavy rains. For vaults, they stacked mats one upon the other. Some acted as the vault, others as the landing area. Dipa continued her training using such makeshift landing mats and pieces of equipment.

Dipa achieved incredible results through her intense training. In 2007, she emerged victorious with five medals at the Junior National Gymnastics Championships. It was a pivotal moment in her life. The medals were proof that she was talented and hardworking. Her coach was convinced that owing to her strength, speed and flexibility, Dipa was ready to compete internationally if she were provided with proper training.

The 2010 Commonwealth Games marked the beginning of Dipa's international journey, where she represented the Indian gymnastics team. Gymnastics involves a predetermined sequence of different moves, beginning with a vault, uneven bars and beam and floor exercises. Dipa's first vault went well, but her hand touched the ground while landing and she lost her balance. This caused her to miss out on a medal.

The setback broke Dipa's heart, but what stung more were the hurtful comments from a fellow gymnast. However, it strengthened her resolve to win the upcoming 2014 Commonwealth Games. Wanting to prove herself, she put her heart and soul into the training.

> Dipa's coach encouraged her to practice the Produnova Vault of Death, famously called so due to its perilous nature and the risk involved in it.

A disparity that women gymnasts in India faced was that the male athletes were given priority to access the facilities. The female gymnasts had to wait patiently for their chance to use the equipment. However, each snub and caustic remark only fuelled Dipa's determination to win an international medal.

A gymnast aiming for an international medal must perform a stunning manoeuvre, so Dipa's coach recommended her to practice the Produnova Vault of Death. The idea sparked a challenging series of practice sessions. With four years until the next Commonwealth Games, her aim was to secure a medal. It required dedication and extensive practice to accomplish the ambitious aim.

The Produnova Vault is famously referred to as the 'Vault of Death' because of its perilous nature. The athlete needs to sprint, launch into the air, perform two somersaults and then land safely on their feet. A single error can cause a gymnast to develop serious injury and become disabled for life.

Maintaining a strict diet and routine, Dipa frequently trained for eight hours daily. She practised the Produnova Vault just three months before the Commonwealth Games. On certain days, her mind was clouded with self-doubt, but her coach was confident of her ability. Dipa rehearsed the vault over a hundred times prior to the competition.

At the 2014 Commonwealth Games in Glasgow, Dipa made history by becoming the first Indian woman gymnast to win a medal. Despite a swollen foot, she performed the Produnova Vault and won the bronze, leaving spectators impressed.

It had taken all of six seconds for Dipa Karmakar to perform the Produnova Vault and win a medal. She smiled and raised her fist in excitement before hurrying off stage to embrace her coach. Her astonishing achievement pulled at the heartstrings of billions of television watchers worldwide. A multitude of honours and awards awaited her upon her return home.

Winning at the Commonwealth Games boosted her self-confidence and made her believe in her ability to perform well on the world stage. With each competition she entered, she emerged victorious and brought home more medals and never looked back. She won a bronze medal at the Asian Gymnastics Championships and the 2015 World Artistic Gymnastics Championships—both were a first for India. The Arjuna Award was bestowed upon Dipa after she returned to India. She was referred to as the gymnastic queen and a star. Even her worst critics acknowledged her as a marvel.

The Produnova Vault catapulted Dipa to fame in the 2016 Rio Olympics. She made history as the first Indian female gymnast in over 50 years to compete in the Olympics and one of just five gymnasts globally to attempt the Produnova Vault.

Despite finishing fourth, her astounding performance captured attention, leading to Dipa being honoured with the prestigious Khel Ratna Award upon her return home.

In 2017, she was honoured with the Padma Shri. Forbes listed her as one of the super achievers under 30 from Asia.

Dipa did not let a knee injury stop her from practising. Her persistence finally paid off when she won a gold medal at the 2018 FIG Artistic Gymnastics World Challenge Cup in Mersin, Turkey, making her the first Indian gymnast to do so.

Dipa loves to watch sports-centric movies and one of her favourites is *Chak De India*, which she has seen multiple times. She enjoys eating Chinese food and ice cream occasionally.

> On Barbie's 60th anniversary, the company chose Dipa Karmakar as a role model and designed a Barbie inspired by the Olympian.

Interestingly, to commemorate Barbie's 60th anniversary in March 2019, the company unveiled a collection of dolls honouring accomplished individuals in various professions. Dipa was chosen as a role model and a Barbie was designed after her to inspire girls around the globe. With its black hair tied in a tight bun, the Barbie sported a mini bronze medal and a red leotard singlet.

In January 2024, Olympian Dipa Karmakar regained her winning form. Eight years after her initial championship win, she reclaimed the title of national champion by capturing three medals including a gold at the Senior Artistic Gymnastics National Championships. On 26 May 2024, Dipa Karmakar made history by becoming the first Indian to win a gold medal in the Asian Senior Championships.

Hockey

1. Historical records show that a primitive version of the game was played in Egypt 4,000 years ago and in Ethiopia since 1000 CE.
2. The history of hockey in India dates to British rule.
3. Hockey was introduced at the 1908 London Olympics, with France, Germany and the four United Kingdom nations taking part.
4. From 1928 to 1956, the Indian hockey team won six Olympic gold medals in a row.
5. Dhyan Chand and his team's remarkable performance in the 1936 Berlin Olympic Games resulted in a crushing 8–1 defeat for Germany, earning India its third consecutive Olympic gold. Dhyan Chand's game impressed Hitler so much that he offered to make him a German army officer in exchange for playing for Germany.
6. The first Indian women's hockey team took part in the Women's Hockey World Cup in Mandelieu, France in March 1974.

P. R. Sreejesh: Indian Hockey's Safe Pair of Hands

The Story

Parattu Raveendran Sreejesh was born on 8 May 1988 in Kizhakkambalam, a small village in the Ernakulam district of Kerala. His father P.V. Raveendran and mother Usha belong to a family of farmers. In his early childhood, Sreejesh wanted to become a pilot as airplanes fascinated him. However, destiny led him to hockey. He studied till class 6 in St Antony's Lower Primary School in Kizhakkambalam and started showing interest in sports during those years. He had a good physique and did well in shot put. When in class 7, he won a prize in shot put at a district-level competition. His performance drew the attention of the right people, and he was offered a chance to go to G.V. Raja Sports School in Thiruvananthapuram, a school that focused on nurturing sports and helping mould champions with character. Several national and international champions, including the Olympians Shiny Wilson and K.M. Beenamol, have been its alumni.

At first, Sreejesh's parents were unwilling to send their 12-year-old 200 kilometres away from home, but considering their son's future they agreed to send him to G.V. Raja Sports School. In hindsight, it was perhaps the best decision they took. Sreejesh's destiny was decided the day he joined the school.

The students of the school played all kinds of sports, and so did Sreejesh. He sprinted, played volleyball and did the long jump. The school's hockey team coaches, Jayakumar and Ramesh Kolappa, noticed his stocky build and body language and encouraged him to play hockey.

At first, Sreejesh, who had never played hockey, was not very keen on the game. However, the thought of standing in one place for goalkeeping seemed less taxing than sprinting, so he obeyed the hockey coaches and began playing the game. He was selected to be the goalkeeper for the school hockey team. To his surprise, he found himself to be good at it.

The turning point in the teenager's life came after he was introduced to Harendra Singh, who was the coach of the Indian junior national hockey team. Soon after, Sreejesh was called for the junior hockey national camp. To attend the camp, he needed to buy a goalkeeper's gear, which cost upwards of 15,000 rupees. His father sold one of the five cows owned by the family and bought him an inexpensive goalkeeper's kit. Equipped with the kit, Sreejesh set out for the camp in Delhi.

> Sreejesh's father sold one of the five cows owned by the family and used the money to buy him his first goalkeeper's kit.

The Journey

Sreejesh had a tough time at the camp at the National Stadium in New Delhi. The thin and cheap pads of his gear were little protection against the merciless balls coming hard and fast, but he continued to brave the assault, trying to save goals. Not knowing Hindi was one of the major challenges for the boy who had never ventured out of Kerala.

The teenager, however, remained dedicated to the purpose for which he had come. He never complained and was determined to do well. He was fit, agile and could bear the pain and dust that came with the game. His school coaches, Jayakumar and Ramesh, had taught him the basics of hockey and showed him how to focus and take his game seriously. He never forgot their advice that a goalkeeper does a thankless job, but he can be the difference between a team winning and losing.

Sreejesh's international debut as a part of the Indian hockey team was in 2004, when he was selected for the national junior team to play against Australia. It was his first international game and did much to boost his confidence. His goalkeeping skills drew the attention of the people in power and two years later, they selected him for the senior Indian team going to play the South Asian Games in Colombo. His excellent goalkeeping during the tournaments saved many goals for the Indian team.

Sreejesh never forgot the goals he conceded during the games at the beginning of his career. The six years he spent sharing matches with senior goalkeepers like Adrian D'Souza, Devesh Chauhan and Bharat Chettri taught him many invaluable lessons. The seniors guided him and helped him handle the pressures while playing at the international level. He followed their moves, watched and learned.

After playing for the senior team, Sreejesh, who was still young enough to play in the junior team, continued to do so. In 2008, he was selected as the goalkeeper for the Indian team in the Junior Asia Cup. In the finals, India beat South Korea 3-2 and bagged the gold medal.

Sreejesh was commended for his astounding performance and was declared the 'Best Goalkeeper of the Tournament'.

Sreejesh became a regular goalkeeper for the Indian hockey team in 2011. In the Men's Asian Champions Trophy in September of the same year in Ordos City, China, Sreejesh helped clinch the gold medal by saving two penalty strokes, and India won the tournament after defeating Pakistan in the final. His contribution to India's victory did not go unnoticed. It earned him the goalkeeper's job for the 2012 London Olympics.

The Indian hockey team's disastrous performance in the London Olympics landed them in the last position. It led to the Indian hockey committee forming a 'Go Young' policy and removing many senior players. Promising young players were taken into the team with the hope of a fresh start. Sreejesh, however, continued to retain his post as the goalkeeper.

A string of victories followed the London Olympics debacle. In the 2013 Men's Hockey Asia Cup finals at Perak, Malaysia, India defeated South Korea 4-3, and qualified for the World Cup to be played in The Hague later in 2014. In the 2014 Asian Games held in Incheon, South Korea, India beat Pakistan in the finals. It was a huge win, as it ended the 16-year wait for a gold medal. Sreejesh was awarded the 'Goalkeeper of the Tournament' for the second time. His dream run as the Indian hockey goalkeeper had begun.

In 2014, India finished second in the Commonwealth Games held in Glasgow and won the silver medal. In 2015, the Indian hockey team won a bronze medal at the International Hockey Federation (FIH) Hockey World League Final. It was their first international medal in 33 years.

In 2015, Sreejesh became the recipient of the Arjuna Award, the only one to get the medal for hockey that year. He led the Indian hockey team in the June 2016 Champions Trophy held in London.

India reached the final but lost to Australia in the final shootout 3-1 and got the silver medal.

Sreejesh also led the Indian hockey team in the 2016 Rio Olympics, his second Olympic games. Although the Indian team could not go beyond the quarterfinals, it was a better performance than the one in London. Besides, Sreejesh put up a fine performance as the goalkeeper. He was called the Great Wall of India.

In January 2017, the Indian government awarded Sreejesh the Padma Shri. This was followed by a difficult phase in his life. In April 2017, he sustained a knee injury during the Sultan Azlan Shah Cup and was forced to take a long break, which cost him the captaincy. He had to undergo two surgeries, and the rehab took a long time. Sreejesh went through an emotional upheaval and even considered retiring from the game for a while. It was the constant encouragement of his family, friends and colleagues that egged him on. His goalkeeper friends Jaap Stockmann of Netherlands, Juan Manuel Vivaldi of Argentina and Kumar Subramaniam of Malaysia joined in the effort and together they convinced him to get back to the game.

> Sreejesh was called the 'Great Wall of India' due to his consistent good performance as the goalkeeper for India at international events.

Sreejesh returned to the game in January 2018 and joined the Indian hockey team for a four-nation tournament in New Zealand. While he was out of action because of injuries, Manpreet Singh Pawar had replaced him as the captain of the team and two other youngsters took turns guarding the goalpost.

The Indian hockey team's performance in the 2017 World Cup held in Bhubaneswar was not impressive. Sreejesh's reflexes had slowed after his injury, and while he made some spectacular saves, India could only reach the quarterfinals. At the 2018 Champions Trophy held in the Netherlands, India lost to Australia in the finals. In the 2019 Sultan Azlan Shah Cup held in Malaysia, India lost to South Korea in the finals. However, the silver medal won by the Indian hockey team qualified them for the 2020 Tokyo Olympics.

There was optimism among the Indian players, and Manpreet Singh Pawar led the Indian hockey team in the Tokyo Olympics in 2021. With less than 7 seconds remaining for the semi-final to end, Sreejesh saved a penalty corner and Germany lost. He was the last line of defence, and he stood like a wall. He held out against the toughest of teams and nullified many attempts to score a goal.

It was the 35-year-old goalkeeper's dazzling performance that brought the Olympics bronze to the country. The bronze medal was more precious than the gold one, coming as it did after 41 years. 2021 was a golden year for Sreejesh. First, he became the second Indian to win the prestigious 'World Games Athlete of the Year' and was also awarded 'Goalkeeper of the Year' by FIH, becoming the third one to win the Goalkeeper of the Year award consecutively.

It is the dream of every athlete to adorn his shelves with an Olympic medal, and Sreejesh had achieved that dream. In his hometown, a road has been named after him as 'Olympian Sreejesh Road'. Sreejesh has also been awarded the Major Dhyan Chand Khel Ratna Award in 2021.

The winning streak for the Indian hockey team continued after the bronze at the Tokyo Olympics. They finished third in the FIH Hockey Pro League, following it up with a silver at the 2022 Birmingham Commonwealth Games with Sreejesh standing like a rock at the goalpost.

Sreejesh works as Joint Director in the Kerala Public Education Department. His favourite hockey players are Dhanraj Pillay, Adrian D'Souza and Baljit Dadwal. A lesser-known fact is that Sreejesh is a voracious reader, who read several books during the COVID-19 lockdown. He is married to Aneeshya, a former long jumper from Kerala, and the couple has two children.

With 300 goals under his belt, Sreejesh's next priority is the 2024 Paris Olympics. Sreejesh has played in three Olympic games and hopes to play in the fourth one too. He believes that though not easy, it is possible to change the colour of the Olympic medal.

Rani Rampal: The Hockey Queen

The Story

Rani Rampal was born on 4 December 1994 to a poor family in the town of Shahabad Markanda, a place notorious for foeticide, in Haryana. Her father was a cart puller and mother a domestic help. Rani was enrolled in school, but her interest lay in the hockey academy nearby. She stood on a side and watched the boys being trained to play hockey. It offered the little girl's mind an escape from the poverty and miseries in her life.

Rani's parents were shocked when she told them about her wish to play hockey. They had never heard of a girl playing any kind of sport. They belonged to a community where girls were expected to stay at home and take care of household chores.

The 6-year-old girl displayed an adamant streak. Her father earned just 80 rupees a day and could just about afford to provide the family with two meals a day. Buying a hockey stick was out of the question, so Rani found a broken hockey stick and started practising.

Every day, she would go around and request Baldev Singh, the hockey coach, to enroll her in his academy. He would laugh and refuse, saying she was not strong enough to pull through a practice session. Baldev Singh's rejection made Rani more determined. She begged her parents to approach the coach, but they brushed her off.

Undeterred, Rani continued to practise with her broken hockey stick. She also continued to pester her parents and the coach till, at last, her parents yielded. They accompanied her to the academy and requested the Dronacharya awardee Baldev Singh to enroll their daughter. Once again, Baldev Singh rejected their request, saying their daughter was too frail to play the energetic game. Thereafter, her father made several rounds of the academy with her in tow.

The exasperated coach told Rani to run a few laps around the field to prove her eligibility. It was her only chance to prove herself, so the little girl put her heart into the task. Baldev Singh was impressed by Rani's agility and agreed to coach her.

Thus, Rani became the youngest player at the Shahabad Hockey Academy.

The Journey

Rani's parents faced a lot of flak from their neighbours and relatives for supporting their daughter's dream. Worried about social boycott, Rani's father insisted that she wear salwar-kameez when she went for practice and Rani agreed.

Baldev Singh was a strict disciplinarian. It was mandatory for each player to bring 500 millilitres of milk, but Rani's parents could only afford 200 millilitres, so she topped the milk with water and carried it to the academy. Despite all setbacks, Rani didn't miss a single day of training.

Baldev Singh was a stickler for punctuality and used to fine any latecomers. The training began very early in the morning, and Rani didn't have a clock at home. One day, Rani reached a few minutes late for practice and Singh asked her to pay a fine of 200 rupees. It was a huge amount for Rani, whose father earned less than 100 rupees a day.

Rani Rampal: The Hockey Queen

When she spoke about the fine at home, Rampal gave her 100 rupees, and she paid the fine. It was an enormous sacrifice for the family.

The coach, who knew about Rani's poverty, returned the amount after adding another 100 rupees to it. Rani was so touched that she vowed never to be late for her practice sessions. Since then, her mother started estimating the time to wake up her daughter by relying on the sun's movement, just like it was done in the old times.

One day, the coach asked Rani to hit a reverse shot and while hitting the shot chickpeas fell out of her pocket. Since snacking was not allowed during the training session, the coach reprimanded her. Rani vowed not to repeat the mistake, no matter how hungry.

Life was tough, and it toughened the girl who was destined for big things. Baldev Singh supported her pursuit of excellence in the game in ways other than training—by buying her hockey kits and shoes and even looking after her dietary needs.

Soon, Rani began taking part in hockey tournaments. She was paid a meagre 500 rupees at a tournament and she gave her earnings to her father. Her gesture touched her father, and his eyes brimmed with tears. An emotional Rani then promised her family that they would have their own home one day.

There was no looking back after that. At 15, Rani became the youngest member of the Indian women's hockey team and played in the Champion's Challenge Tournament held in Kazan, Russia. She

> At 15, Rani became the youngest member of the Indian women's hockey team and played in the Champion's Challenge Tournament in Russia.

stunned the spectators by striking four goals and became the top goal scorer. The innocent teenager did not know about the importance of the tournament.

The tournament was a precursor of Rani's achievements. The next year, she was a part of the FIH Women's All-Star team and All-Star team of the Asian Hockey Federation in 2010. She played in the Asian and Commonwealth Games the same year.

She was the youngest player in the national team which took part in the 2010 World Cup in Canada. She achieved a stupendous 7-goal score in the tournament as India finished 9th in the World Women's hockey rankings. It was the Indian women's hockey team's best performance since 1978.

Money was still an issue for Rani. Her father still pulled his cart, and Rani's hockey kits and nutritional supplements were costly. This was when her seniors stepped in by helping in various ways.

At 18, she scored three goals (one in regulation time, one in the shoot-out and one in sudden death) against England in Mönchengladbach, Germany, and India won its first-ever bronze medal at the Junior World Cup. This brought her the reputation of a sudden death goal expert.

Once Rani began playing professionally, a sports NGO called GoSports Foundation started supporting her as her family found it hard to support her dreams financially.

Shahabad Markanda, which had hitherto been known for excellent male hockey players like Gurdeep Singh Bhullar and Sandeep Singh, was now known for Rani Rampal. The town, which didn't allow girls to go out alone, which was against her taking up hockey, was now surging with ambitious girls who wanted to emulate her example.

Rani's wins brought her some rewards and a modest job in the railways, but nothing changed at home. Her father continued to pull his cart and provide for the family, as always. Her brothers continued to work as carpenters.

The Indian women's hockey team did not make it through the qualifying rounds for the 2012 London Olympics. The opportunity to play in the Olympics came to the Indian team after 36 years in the 2016 Rio Olympics. It was a breakthrough even though the team failed to bring back a medal.

Rani received the Arjuna Award in 2016. She led the Indian women's hockey team as captain in the 2018 Asian Games, where they won a silver medal and Rani was India's flag bearer for the closing ceremony of the games. She became the first-ever hockey player to be given the prestigious 'World Games Athlete of the Year' award in 2019.

The admirable part of Rani's game is the ability to score under pressure. Her performance and perseverance have inspired the girls in blue to give their best to the game. Rani was awarded the Padma Shri in 2020 in recognition of her excellent contribution to the national hockey team. The same year she became the first woman hockey player and only the third from the sport to receive the Khel Ratna, India's highest sporting honour.

In the qualifying rounds for the Tokyo Olympics, being held in Bhubaneswar, Rani made sure that her team entered the games by scoring the crucial goal against USA in the final qualification

> Rani became the first-ever hockey player to be honoured with the prestigious 'World Games Athlete of the Year' award in 2019.

match. That goal took the Indian women's hockey team to Tokyo in 2021, but they lost to Great Britain in the bronze medal play-off. Once again, the team returned without winning a medal, but they had created history by reaching the semi-finals and winning many hearts.

In March 2023, the hockey stadium at the Indian Railways' Modern Coach Factory (MCF) in Rae Bareli was renamed as 'Rani's Girls Hockey Turf'. This was an unprecedented honour, and Rani became the first Indian sportswoman to have a stadium named after her.

Rani has the distinction of playing in 250 international matches. No Indian woman has played more internationals nor scored as many goals. Her goals have resulted in many medals, gold and silver, for the country.

From playing with a broken hockey stick to leading the Indian women's team to the Olympics, Rani has come a long way. The girl, who idolizes Dhanraj Pillay, is living her dream. She has finally built the dream house she had promised her family.

Shooting

1. The National Rifle Association (NRA) is the oldest shooting association in the world.
2. The Olympic Games comprise 15 shooting events, divided into pistol, rifle and shotgun categories. The events have been further divided based on their distance. There are two rounds in every event—the qualification and the finals.
3. The shotgun event in the Olympics is the oldest shooting event and the only one with a moving target. The two shotgun events are trap and skeet.
4. In the past, pigeons were used as targets, but now clay is used. The scoring system is simple: it's either a hit or a miss. Interestingly, the shotgun has the longest and the shortest distance events in shooting.
5. Trap has the greatest aiming distance, while skeet has the least. In a trap, the shooter must aim in the air. They are not informed about the direction of the target. The clay target can be released from any of the three areas.
6. The International Shooting Sport Federation (ISSF), founded in 1907, is the governing body of the Olympics shooting events.

4 GOLDS IN A ROW

CWG
2002
2006
2010
2014

ABHINAV Bindra

SHOOTING

Abhinav Bindra: The Man with the Golden Gun

The Story

Abhinav was born on 28 September 1982 in Dehradun, Uttarakhand, to a wealthy Punjabi family. His father, Apjit Bindra, is a successful businessman, and his mother, Babli, a descendant of Maharaja Hari Singh's family, was an active sportsperson during her youth and a major influence in Abhinav's life.

The young boy was no stranger to guns. His father owned three of them and gifted Abhinav his first air gun on his tenth birthday. Abhinav began by shooting at bottles, which he continued to reduce in size as the days passed. Observing his son's interest in shooting, Apjit consulted his friend, Rana Gurmeet Sodhi, who was the sports minister. The minister suggested the name of Lieutenant Colonel Jagir Singh Dhillon as a coach for Abhinav. A letter from Abhinav, who promised to make the colonel proud of him, made the colonel accept the challenge and Abhinav's coaching started in a makeshift range under a mango tree. Soon thereafter, his parents built a 10-metre shooting range in their house so he could practice whenever he wanted.

Abhinav attended the Doon School in Dehradun and St. Stephen's School in Chandigarh. His mother employed the services of Amit Bhattacharjee, a teacher who later became a friend and coach to Abhinav.

It was a tight schedule for the boy, who would attend school and then rush off for his training with Colonel Dhillon. When most children enjoyed their after-school hours playing or chatting, Abhinav practised shooting. Then he also had to finish his homework and study. Starting with 21 hours a week, his training hours grew longer, leaving him no time for other pursuits. It was a difficult routine, but he did not complain.

His dedication and hard work paid off when, at 13, Abhinav won his first medal at the Ropar District Shooting Competition. The medal was a testimony to his shooting skill. It boosted the teenager's confidence and motivated him to achieve bigger success.

The Journey

Abhinav broke the world record by scoring 200/200 at the Junior State Championship 1996 in Patiala. Unfortunately, the competition was not recognized by the ISSF. Later that year, at the qualifying event for the Nationals, when Abhinav scored 400/400, the authorities refused to believe that the 14-year-old boy could have performed the feat. However, it was alleged that the bullets used during the event were not as per the ISSF norms. Abhinav wasn't cowed by it. Finally, the allegation was proved wrong, and the embarrassed authorities ordered a re-shoot for him to qualify. The teenager had the last laugh when he qualified in the re-shoot and later won the bronze medal at the Nationals held in Asansol.

Abhinav's goal was set. He wanted to take part in the Olympic Games, and there was no looking back. Crossing the hurdles, he progressed toward his dream. At 15, he was the youngest competitor in the 1998 Commonwealth Games in Kuala Lumpur, Malaysia. His dream of taking part in the Olympic Games came true when, in 2000, he became the youngest Indian athlete to compete in the Sydney Olympics.

In 2002, Abhinav won six gold medals at various events and won a bronze, setting a record score in junior shooting at the World Cup. He won gold in the 10-metre air rifle pairs and silver in the singles at the 2002 Commonwealth Games in Manchester.

He has represented India in five Olympic games, in 2000, 2004, 2008, 2012 and 2016, winning a medal only once in 2008. In 2000, he set a junior shooting record but failed to win a medal. In the 2004 Athens Olympics, he made it to the finals and came very close to winning a medal.

After the Athens Olympics, when preparations for the Beijing Olympics began, Abhinav suffered from severe back pain. The pain was so severe that he could not even lift his rifle. To take part in the Olympics, he had to qualify the 2006 ISSF World Shooting Championships. Abhinav went through extensive therapy. He bagged a gold medal in the 10-metre air rifle event at the ISSF World Shooting Championships held in Zagreb in 2006.

> In 2002, Abhinav won six gold medals and one bronze at various events, and set a record score in junior shooting at the World Cup.

It was thanks to his determination and the help of his German coach couple, Heinz Reinkemeier and Gaby, that he made a strong comeback and qualified for the Beijing Olympics. A week before the games Abhinav underwent commando training with his consultant coach, Uwe Riesterer. It was an exercise in stress management.

Riesterer, a commando, led him through a series of thrilling tasks: crossing a wooden log over a 50-60-foot chasm, climbing a rock-climbing wall and, most fascinatingly, ascending a 40-foot pizza pole, which derives its name from the platform at the peak, which is the size of a pizza box.

In the finals of the men's 10-metre air rifle at the 2008 Beijing Games, Abhinav was tied with Henri Hakkinen of Finland for the gold, with one shot remaining. He scored 10.8 and won the gold and finally realized his childhood dream.

It was a victory not only for him, but for all those who believed in him—his family, coaches and friends. It was a victory that had come 60 years after the first Olympic medal, and it was the first individual Olympic medal won by an Indian. Accolades, honours and congratulatory messages followed the victory. He was not just a national, but an international celebrity, and Abhinav realized the true meaning of stardom.

Though a shooter must have sharp eyesight, Abhinav used to shoot with a -3 vision and almost no peripheral vision. In 2008, after his historic win in the Beijing Olympics, the shooter went through surgery to correct his peripheral vision.

After Abhinav's success in the 2008 Beijing Olympics, having achieved his lifelong dream, he was a bit lost. So much so that he toyed with the idea of giving up the sport and retiring. Fortunately after a year of indecision, he finally returned to shooting.

In the 2010 Commonwealth Games held in Delhi, Abhinav had the honour of being the flag bearer for the opening ceremony and also taking the athletes' oath on behalf of the 6,700 participants from 71 countries and territories. Abhinav, along with Gagan Narang, another ace shooter from India, partnered to win gold in the 10-metre air rifle (Pairs) event.

Abhinav followed it up by winning a silver medal in the 2010 Asian Games in Guangzhou, China. He took part in the 2012 London Olympics but missed reaching the finals.

Another setback followed the London debacle. Diagnosed with epilepsy, Abhinav struggled with tremors in his left hand in 2014. He went for treatment under the sports medicine specialist Hans-Wilhelm Muller-Wohlfahrt. It was a tough time, but he overcame the challenge and won a gold medal in the 2014 Glasgow Commonwealth Games. A bronze in the Incheon Asian Games followed the same year.

Participating in the 2016 Rio Olympics was a proud moment for the shooter, who was designated as the goodwill ambassador and flag bearer. However, just before the event, the 'sight' of his rifle broke. He and his coach had created the sight especially for Rio and did not have a replacement. It shook him, just as it would any shooter. Abhinav missed the third position by a mere 0.1 point.

At 34, soon after the Rio Olympics, he announced his retirement. After a shooting career spanning 22 years, Abhinav retired on 5 September 2016. The country will always remember him for winning India's first individual gold medal in the Olympics.

Besides the much-coveted medals, Abhinav has been honoured with many awards. In 2000, he was awarded the Arjuna Award, and the Rajiv Gandhi Khel Ratna was conferred on him in 2001. In 2008, the ISSF honoured him with the Blue Cross, which is their highest shooting award. The Padma Bhushan was bestowed on him in 2009. In 2011, the Indian Territorial Army appointed him and gave him the rank of honorary Lieutenant Colonel. In 2011, he authored *A Shot at History: My Obsessive Journey to Olympic Gold*, along with sports writer Rohit Brijnath, an account of his life, challenges and career. In 2019, SRM and Kaziranga University felicitated him with honorary doctorate degrees in literature and philosophy.

After retirement, he decided to give back to his favourite sport. He offers financial help to promising young shooters through the Abhinav Bindra Shooting Development Programme. He is the CEO of Abhinav Futuristics Limited, which is the only company in the country to sell Walther's brand of pistols. He is a board member of the GoSports Foundation. He also started the Abhinav Bindra Foundation, a non-profit organization that looks after the all-around development of athletes using modern sports technology and techniques.

Since 2010, Abhinav has been a member of the Sports Committee of the Federation of Indian Chambers of Commerce and Industry (FICCI). He was part of the ISSF, the International Olympic Committee (IOC)'s Athlete Commissions, where he raised issues related to participants, their problems and hardships to improve their all-around development and performance.

Abhinav is an inspiration for all sports enthusiasts and aspirants.

> Abhinav Futuristics Limited, of which Abhinav Bindra is the CEO, is the only company in the country to sell Walther's brand of pistols.

Weightlifting

1. Weightlifting was practised in ancient India, China, Egypt and Greece.
2. The development of weightlifting as an international sport primarily took place during the 19th century. It was one of the sports featured at the first modern Olympic Games in Athens in 1896.
3. The first International Women's Tournament took place in Budapest, Hungary in March 1986.
4. While weightlifting for men has a long history, women's weightlifting debuted in the Olympic Games in 2000 in Sydney.
5. Karnam Malleswari was the first Indian woman to win an Olympic medal.

Achinta Sheuli: The Determined Weightlifter

The Story

Achinta was born on 24 November 2001 in Pratik and Purnima Sheuli's tiny shanty in Deulpur, West Bengal. Pratik was a daily-wage labourer, who struggled to feed the four members of the family. His wife helped by taking up whatever job came her way. Life was tough for the family, with low-paying jobs, a run-down house and not enough to eat.

Achinta's brother, Alok, was seven years elder to him and his role model. The two brothers attended Deulpur High School. Alok was keen on pursuing weightlifting and went regularly to the home-gym run by Astam Das. He took 10-year-old Achinta to the gym to make him more confident.

The two boys began going to Astam Das's modest home-gym, where he trained village children without charging any fee. Most of his pupils came from very poor families and did not have a balanced diet, much less multivitamins or supplements. They often practised under a tree when it was not raining. The tin-roofed veranda in his dilapidated brick house was used for practising with barbells.

Tragedy struck the family when Achinta's father died in 2013. The grieving boys did not have money even to cremate their father and had to borrow from relatives and friends to perform the last rites.

After his father's death, Achinta's mother struggled to put food on the table. She worked as a help and took up embroidery work. But still it was not enough for them to eat two square meals a day. Both Alok and Achinta helped with the embroidery work, which was painstaking and brought very little money. To make ends meet, Alok quit college and took up any odd job that came his way. Achinta worked alongside, but he did not give up weightlifting. His brother's words that a medal in the sport could be his ticket out of penury struck a chord with him. Convinced that it was the only escape route from his circumstances, he began practising harder.

Soon, Achinta was practising for about two-and-a-half hours every day after school. Besides helping their mother with the zari work, the two boys also hauled big loads for a pittance. They would work in the fields and carry rice sacks in return for eggs or chicken so that they could eat protein.

Achinta lifted weights from 9 a.m. to 10 a.m. without eating anything. He would then go home and eat a bit before going to school. He returned at 4 p.m., ate *phena bhaat* (rice congee) and a hard-boiled egg and went back to training. He would train till 7 p.m. and return home. But he was determined to lift the family out of the morass. His coach, Astam Das, supplemented his dietary needs when he noticed him training extra hard.

The hard work soon resulted in success. It was 2013, just two months after their father's death, when both Alok and Achinta took part in their first national, which was being held in Guwahati. While Achinta took part in the 50 kg category and was placed fourth in the competition, Alok took part in the 69 kg category and found himself in the eighth place.

The opportunity Achinta had been waiting for arrived then. Officials of the ASI noted his performance and offered him a chance to join the institute in Pune. That was the turning point in his life.

The Journey

Joining the Boys Sports Company at the ASI in Pune was the best thing that happened to Achinta Sheuli. Not only did he get the training to take part in national and international sports competitions, but he also got a balanced and nutritious diet and an education as per the CBSE pattern.

The training and food at the ASI helped Achinta become strong and skilled. He was now ready for better things. In 2015, he won a silver medal in the Commonwealth Youth Championships held in Apia, Samoa and in 2018, he won a gold medal in the Khelo India Youth Games, held in New Delhi. The Indian Army granted him the rank of havildar, improving the family's circumstances.

In 2015, Achinta won a silver medal in the Commonwealth Youth Championships held in Samoa. He won a gold in the Khelo India Youth Games in 2018.

Medals dotted his path to success as Achinta won a gold medal in the 2019 Commonwealth Senior and Junior Championships. Another gold came his way the same year in the South Asian Games held in Kathmandu. He went on to win a silver in the Asian Youth Championships held in Gifu, Japan, and one in the 2021 Junior World Championships held in Tashkent.

The historic win came at the Birmingham Commonwealth Games 2022, where Achinta set a record by lifting 170 kg in the clean-and-jerk series and 143 in the snatch, totalling 313 kg. Congratulatory messages poured in from all parts of the country. Right from Prime Minister Narendra Modi and President Droupadi Murmu to the West Bengal Chief Minister Mamata Banerjee, everyone greeted the young man who had brought glory to the nation.

Achinta dedicated his award to his brother who sacrificed his weightlifting career for his family. On his homecoming, the whole village was jubilant and a constant stream of relatives, friends and neighbours flowed through the house, congratulating him. Notwithstanding his success, Achinta retains his shyness. He's a reserved person who has remained grounded and not forgotten his humble beginnings.

> Achinta created history at the Birmingham Commonwealth Games 2022, where he set a record by lifting 170 kg in the clean-and-jerk series and 143 in the snatch.

Jeremy Lalrinnunga: The Prodigious Weightlifter

The Story

Jeremy Lalrinnunga was born on 26 October 2002 in the picturesque town of Aizwal in Mizoram. His father, Lalneihtluanga, was a pugilist and a well-known name in the Mizoram boxing circle. He had won two gold medals at the national sub-junior level and dreamed of representing the country in the international forum one day. However, he had to lay aside his gloves to look after his family. But he decided to train his five sons so they could attain their dreams. Although he wanted his sons to become athletes, he allowed them to choose the sport they preferred.

Inspired by their father, the boys began training in boxing. Jeremy was 8 when he began going to his father's boxing academy and impressed everyone with his prowess. Unfortunately, the boxing academy closed down because of financial troubles. It so happened that the little boy saw his friends lifting weights at the village gym and was quite awestruck.

He requested Malsawma Khiangte, the weightlifting coach at SYS (Department of Sports and Youth Services) to train him. Malsawma asked Jeremy to bring a bamboo and then to lift it slowly. Those sticks were 5 metres long and 20 millimetres wide. There was no weight on them, but it is tougher to lift a stick than weights, because one needs to know the technique of balancing it. Jeremy practised day and night, lifting bamboo sticks and learning the art of balancing. It is important to learn the basic techniques before one is trained in weightlifting and so Jeremy's weightlifting training began with the 'bamboo technique'. It improved his focus, too. It was only after he had learned to balance the sticks that he was allowed to lift weights.

According to coach Malsawma, Jeremy's strong shoulders and back muscles distinguished him from the other kids and his technique, particularly in snatch, was good. Eight months of rigorous training later, the coach suggested Jeremy should try to enroll himself in the ASI, Pune. Jeremy was one of the three boys selected for training at the ASI. He was 9 years old when his training began in earnest.

> Jeremy practised day and night, lifting bamboo sticks and learning the art of balancing. This also helped improve his focus.

The Journey

While there was jubilation in Jeremy's family about the ASI selection, there was also anxiety. The boy had never been away from the family and could communicate only in Mizo, but those challenges could not deter him from his path. In September 2012, Jeremy joined the Boys Sports Company at the ASI and started specialized training in weightlifting. It didn't take long for the cheerful boy to overcome the language barrier. At ASI, Jeremy began training under a new coach, Zarzokema, who was also from Mizoram.

Jeremy's family was poor. His father, Lalneihtluanga, was a contract labourer with the PWD. Sometimes when he used to come home on a break, they could barely afford his return ticket to Pune.

Fortunately, Jeremy was unstoppable. He had found an aim and was working steadily towards it. His first medal was a gold at the sub-junior nationals in Patna, which he followed up with a silver medal at the World Youth Weightlifting Championships. He was just 13 years old and the second youngest weightlifter to compete. After bagging a silver at the 2017 World Youth Championships, he followed it up with a silver and a bronze at the 2018 Asian Youth Championships. His excellent performance in the World Youth Weightlifting Championships won him a berth in the prestigious 2018 Youth Olympics in Buenos Aires, Argentina.

Living up to the country's expectations, he set a record by becoming the first Indian to win a gold medal at the Youth Olympics. In the Asian Youth Championships 2019, he set a national record with a lift of 306 kg in the 67 kg category.

In May 2019, Jeremy joined the army as a Naib Subedar. He now had the dual responsibility of being a soldier and a sportsperson. Upholding the nation's honour was now his primary responsibility.

However, life didn't get any easier. Injuries and pain resulted in lost opportunities for Jeremy. Just after the Youth Olympics, he was diagnosed with a cyst in the knee, which had to be removed with surgery. It was a frustrating time as the injury halted his training for a while. There were endless sessions of physiotherapy and strengthening exercises. This resulted in a dip in Jeremy's performance. His 4th place finish at the qualifying event resulted in his missing out on the Tokyo Olympics 2020.

After winning no medals for almost a year, Jeremy finally won gold at the Commonwealth Games in December 2021. However, Jeremy's

Jeremy Lalrinnunga: The Prodigious Weightlifter

troubles were far from over. A spinal injury just a few months before the 2022 Commonwealth Games sent his coach into a tizzy, but the champion was not giving up. He was determined to win a medal at the games. To motivate himself, he used an image of a Commonwealth Games gold medal as wallpaper on his phone.

Wallpapers, however inspiring, do not bring medals. Only hard work, continuous practice and firm determination can do that and Jeremy ensured he kept up with the three factors. His self-belief and positivity continued to be his strengths and nothing can defeat a person with those qualities. Soon, a combination of therapy, pain management and willpower saw Jeremy recover in time to compete in the 2022 Commonwealth Games in Birmingham.

Jeremy's first shot in the clean-and-jerk attempt (154 kg) resulted in a cramp in his thigh. There was a sharp intake of collective breath as he fell to the floor, writhing in pain. A few minutes later, he attempted to lift 160 kg, 6 kg more than his earlier attempt. Some would consider the move foolhardy, but Jeremy was determined to better his personal record.

Struggling with pain, he hoisted the weight successfully and then he let out a loud roar and collapsed to the ground once again. The worried look on the face of Vijay Sharma, Jeremy's coach, said it all. The young man was writhing in pain and had to be helped away from the stage.

> A combination of therapy, pain management and willpower saw Jeremy recover in time to compete in the 2022 Commonwealth Games.

Jeremy had set a record with a total lift of 300 kg—140 kg in snatch and 160 kg in clean and jerk. He could have stopped. Yet, he returned to the podium once again, this time to lift 165 kg in clean and jerk, almost two-and-a-half times his body weight. It was a challenge for someone as diminutive as Jeremy, but he tried to achieve the impossible. This time, his elbows gave way and he fell writhing to the floor. He didn't pull off the feat, but the world acknowledged the grit and determination of the gold medal winner.

The teenager was applauded for his superman feat, but the best gesture came from Vaipava Loane, the silver medal winner, who placed his traditional Samoan red-coloured garland around Jeremy's neck as a mark of respect.

In Mizoram, his family and friends erupted in jubilation as they watched Jeremy's accomplishment. Malsawma Khiangte, who was Jeremy's first coach, beamed with happiness at his pupil's success. Headlines across the world hailed the teenager's courage and determination. Media gushed over the champion's achievement and congratulatory messages poured in. From his blonde-tipped hairstyle to the tattoos, the media highlighted every element of his personality.

In 2023, Jeremy won a silver medal in the snatch category at the Asian Weightlifting Championships held in Jinju, South Korea.

Despite all the swag and confidence, Jeremy is a simple, down-to-earth person. He is also a responsible son and shares a close bond with his four brothers, who are all boxers.

1ST INDIAN WOMAN TO WIN AN OLYMPIC MEDAL

Karnam Malleswari

WEIGHTLIFTING

Karnam Malleswari: The Stellar Weightlifter

The Story

Karnam Malleswari was born on 1 June 1975 in a small village called Voosavanipeta in Andhra Pradesh. She was one of the five daughters of Ramdas and Shyamala Karnam. Her father worked as a constable in the Railway Protection Force. Malleswari and her sisters were blessed with powerful muscles, which did not escape the eyes of a weightlifting coach, who suggested to her parents that the girls should take up weightlifting.

At the time, weightlifting was a male-dominated sport, so her father was not in favour of his daughters taking it up. Even relatives advised the girls against weightlifting. It was Shyamala, Malleswari's mother, who encouraged the daughters to take up the sport. Her only condition was that the girls take it seriously and achieve success.

Malleswari's sisters joined the local gymnasium near their school in Voosavanipeta in Andhra Pradesh and took up weightlifting under coach Neelamshetty Appanna. Malleswari's aspiration to join the gym at 12 was met with scepticism by the coach, who felt she was too thin for weightlifting. Her mother encouraged her to prove him wrong. When Malleswari first started lifting weights, she had to overcome the lack of coaching and equipment, relying solely on her own motivation. Despite his initial reluctance, the coach finally gave in to the girl's determination and allowed her to join her sisters in weightlifting training.

With no weightlifting kits, Malleswari and her sisters had to get creative with their training. The girls practised on the muddy field, using the local barbell that had been worn down and bent from years of use. They would find a way to make it straight and continue their practice. They did not even know that weightlifters needed specialized shoes and belts.

In the early days, the girls had no sponsors and had to make the most of their limited resources. They opted for inexpensive hostels or dharamshalas to save money. Since eating out was not an option, Malleswari's mother came along on the tours with a gas stove and utensils. She would purchase vegetables from the nearby market and cook for them at the dharamshala where they were staying.

> Malleswari impressed the Olympic and world champion Leonid Taraneko by lifting 35 kg, which was equivalent to her body weight.

The turning point came when Malleswari tagged along with her elder sister Krishna Kumari to the SAI's national camp. She was keenly observing the weightlifters when she was noticed by the Olympic and world champion, Leonid Taraneko. He asked her if she was interested in the sport. When Malleswari nodded, he asked her to lift. To his surprise, she lifted around 35 kg, which was equivalent to her body weight. He was so impressed that he recommended her to the Bangalore Sports Institute. For the next 11 months, Taraneko taught her the technical aspects of weightlifting and that was the launch of her successful career.

The Journey

Malleswari was a girl on a mission to see the Indian flag fly high while the national anthem played at the world stage. In the 1990 junior national weightlifting championships at Udaipur, the 15-year-old Malleswari left the crowd in awe as she demolished nine records in the 52 kg division. The following year, she made her mark by earning a silver medal in the senior national championships, which took place in Ambala. Next, she proudly brought back a bronze medal from the 1993 World Championships held in Melbourne.

After a year of intense training, she exceeded expectations and secured the top spot, winning gold at the 1994 World Championships in Istanbul. Amidst the thunderous cheers and applause, Malleswari stood proudly on the podium. Her heart swelled with joy as she clutched the gleaming gold medal, a historic first for our country. A silver at the 1994 Asian Games, Hiroshima joined her list of medals. In the 1995 World Championships held in China, she triumphed once again, winning another gold medal.

By the year 2000, out of her 29 international medals, 11 were gold. In 2000, the Sydney Olympic Games made history by including the women's weightlifting event for the first time. Malleswari flew to Sydney hoping to emerge victorious and claim a medal at the event, though there wasn't much expectation in general.

In the finals, Malleswari was competing with Hungary's Erzsebet Markus and China's Lin Weining. All three lifted 110 kg in the snatch event. In the clean-and-jerk event both her competitors lifted 132.5 kg. Malleswari attempted to lift 137.5 kg, but could not hold as she lifted

Karnam Malleswari: The Stellar Weightlifter

the barbell a little too quickly. Though she missed gold, Malleswari made history by winning a bronze medal in her first trip to the games, becoming the first Indian woman to achieve an Olympic medal. Back home, as soon as they learned of her victory, her parents, friends and relatives erupted in cheers and celebration.

Thousands of people applauded and garlanded her as Malleswari stepped out of the airport on reaching India. Prime Minister Atal Bihari Vajpayee called to congratulate her on the victory. He used the term '*Bharat ki beti*' (daughter of India) to address her.

Karnam Malleswari's success inspired countless Indian girls to dream of earning medals. Mahavir Phogat was inspired to train his daughters for wrestling after watching Malleswari on TV in 2000.

> Prime Minister Vajpayee used the term '*Bharat ki beti*' (daughter of India) to address Malleswari after her Olympic win in 2000.

The Government of India recognized her achievements with prestigious awards like the Arjuna Award in 1994, Rajiv Gandhi Khel Ratna in 1999 and Padma Shri in 1999.

Malleswari hopes to inspire many young people to embrace weightlifting and bring back a gold medal from the Olympic Games. Keeping that in mind, she has set up the Karnam Malleswari Foundation in Yamunanagar.

In June 2021, Karnam Malleswari was appointed the vice-chancellor of Delhi Sports University. She aspires to foster talent and inspire young individuals to pursue sports.

Mirabai Chanu: Miracle Mira

The Story

Born on 8 August 1994 in Nongpok Kakching, a village in Imphal, Mirabai grew up in a humble environment. She was the youngest among the six children of Saikhom Kriti Meitei and Saikohm Tombi Leima. While her father was employed with the Public Works Department (PWD), her mother ran a tea stall to supplement the family's earnings. Despite the limited resources available, Mirabai's parents encouraged their children to dream big and have ambition.

As a child, Mirabai would carry drums of water on her head over uneven terrain as there was no water source near her house. The rainy season made the already terrible conditions even worse, as the tracks became slick and unsafe. Sometimes, she would manage to carry a large bundle of firewood, which her older brother could not even lift, at the age of 12. At the time, her brother, Sanatomba, joked that Mira could become a weightlifter.

Mirabai's dream of becoming an athlete took root when she was young. She was interested in archery, a popular sport in Manipur. At 14, she made her way to a nearby archery centre to enroll in training. Much to her surprise, the centre was closed that day. But she watched the weightlifters who were practising nearby. She was impressed by their muscular arms and their ability to lift heavy weights. Thus, she became completely enthralled by the sport. Although she could lift heavy things, weightlifting was not something she had considered.

Soon after, she learned about Kunjarani Devi, the highly decorated Indian weightlifter, whose journey was both inspiring as well as extremely relatable for Mirabai, as she found several parallels between both their lives. Interestingly, Kunjarani had a huge role to play later as she coached Mirabai.

The Journey

The nearest weightlifting training centre was over 30 kilometres from Mirabai's house and there was no regular bus service from her place to the training centre. The solution came in the form of trucks that passed through her village, carrying sand to the town. The drivers often halted at her mother's tea stall for a break. Mirabai decided to request the truck drivers for a ride. Every day she would find a kind truck driver who would let her hitchhike to the city. And so began her training at the Khuman Lampak Sports Complex in Imphal.

Despite many hurdles, Mirabai focused on her training. The hardships of her early life provided her with the strength and discipline required by an athlete.

> Mirabai leaped into the international circuit in the 2014 Commonwealth Games, where she won a silver medal. She won a gold in the 2017 World Championships.

She opened her medal account with a national medal in the junior category and leaped into the international circuit in the 2014 Commonwealth Games, where she won a silver medal. The next step was to win a medal in the Olympics and she began practising for the Rio Olympics. She did not even attend her sister's wedding because she was focusing on her training. However, at the Rio Olympics, Mirabai failed to lift the weights and had to bow out of the competition. It was a big blow to her morale. The failure hit her hard, so much so that she considered quitting. However, timely counsel by the psychologists at the SAI helped her resume her training.

Mirabai's mother and her coach, Vijay Sharma, also played a crucial role in her recovery. She immersed herself in intense training sessions and won a gold medal in the 2017 World Championships, followed by gold in the 2018 Commonwealth Games.

On 24 July 2021, at the Tokyo Olympics, Mirabai achieved a historic milestone by winning India's first-ever Olympic silver medal in weightlifting. Her incredible feat made her the first Indian in 21 years to secure a weightlifting medal, after Karnam Malleswari, who secured a bronze medal in weightlifting at the 2000 Sydney Olympic Games.

Mirabai's win gave Indians everywhere a cause for celebration. Congratulatory messages poured in from all corners. There were numerous articles written by journalists about the Iron Woman from Manipur. People were curious about the woman who, despite weighing only 49 kg, had managed to lift a massive 202 kg weight to win the medal. She began to be popularly referred to as 'Miracle Mira'.

Interestingly, her immediate desire after her magnificent victory was to eat a pizza as it had been a long time since she had eaten one. Upon learning this, Dominos announced that they would provide her with free pizzas for life. Mirabai's first act upon returning home was to invite the truck drivers for a meal and express her gratitude for the support they provided during her early training.

In 2018, Mirabai was honoured with the country's highest sporting award, Rajiv Gandhi Khel Ratna, and also the Padma Shri. A play based on her life story was adapted in the Meitei language and released in September 2021.

Mirabai bagged another gold medal in the 2022 Birmingham Commonwealth Games. She serves as an inspiration for athletes from across borders. Nooh Dastagir Butt attributes his success as Pakistan's first Commonwealth Games gold medallist to the cheerful weightlifter. Mirabai won a gold in the women's 49 kg weightlifting competition at the 2022 National Games in November.

Despite her success, she remains unfazed and continues to strive for greater heights. The 2024 Olympic Games in Paris is her next goal, where she plans to earn a gold medal. Prior to that, she wants to address the shoulder injuries she's been enduring. Mirabai aspires to teach weightlifting to the children in her village and motivate young girls everywhere to have big dreams and pursue them with unwavering determination.

> Mirabai serves as an inspiration for athletes from across borders. Pakistan's Nooh Dastagir Butt attributes his success to the cheerful weightlifter.

Wrestling

1. The history of wrestling goes back even before 3000 BCE. Cave drawings from ancient times depict wrestling moves and techniques that are still practised.
2. References to wrestling can also be found in several old texts, such as the Old Testament, the Vedas and ancient texts of Sanskrit literature.
3. 'Malla yuddha', an ancient form of wrestling in India, finds mention in ancient Hindu epics like the Ramayana and the Mahabharata.
4. In the Mahabharata, among the Pandava brothers, Bhima, famous for his strength, was highly skilled in the art of wrestling. He took part in a wrestling match with the well-known wrestler Jarasandha.
5. Each civilization developed its distinct form of wrestling. Kushti was the unique wrestling style practised by Indian wrestlers. The Japanese are famous for their tradition of Sumo wrestling. The ancient Greeks brought grappling to Olympic wrestling.
6. Ancient Greek Olympic Games included wrestling as one of the sports.
7. Wrestling was first featured at the Olympics in 1896.

8. Prior to Athens 2004, only men's events were part of the programme, but after four years, four categories for women were also introduced.
9. For Paris 2024, Olympic wrestling features 18 weight classes—6 each for men's freestyle, women's freestyle and Greco-Roman.
10. Men's Freestyle: 57 kg, 65 kg, 74 kg, 86 kg, 97 kg, 125 kg.
11. Women's Freestyle: 50 kg, 53 kg, 57 kg, 62 kg, 68 kg, 76 kg.
12. Greco-Roman (Men's): 60 kg, 67 kg, 77 kg, 87 kg, 97 kg, 130 kg.

4 WORLD CHAMPIONSHIP MEDALS

- 2013
- 2018
- 2019
- 2022

BAJRANG Punia

WRESTLING

Bajrang Punia: A Lion in the Ring

The Story

Bajrang Punia was born on 26 February 1994 in Khuddan village of Jhajjar, Haryana. He is the youngest in a family of three siblings. His father, Balwan Singh Punia, and mother, Om Pyari Punia, belonged to poor Jat families. They named him 'Bajrang' after Lord Hanuman, the Hindu god who is worshipped for his unrivalled strength. He is worshipped by countless devotees every Tuesday. Since Bajrang was born on a Tuesday, he was thus named after Lord Hanuman. However, the parents did not know their son would live up to the name one day.

Khuddan has very few sports facilities and children take to inexpensive sports like kabaddi or wrestling. A mud *akhara* (wrestling ring) does not cost much and *dangal* promises a good sport. As a result, every second family in the village has a wrestler or two. Almost every boy's birth heralds yet another wrestler. Competitive bouts are a common occurrence and bring some prize money, too. To be a good *pehalwan* is a matter of great pride for many young men.

Bajrang's father and brothers took pride in being wrestlers. It was a given that all the sons would take up the sport. Bajrang followed his elder brother into the mud pit of the *akhara* to watch him wrestle with the other boys in the village. Since he was 7, he began taking part in the bouts, wrestling with boys older than him.

Bajrang's father was surprised to see his son wrestling for the first time. The little boy took part in six consecutive bouts and was raring for more. Soon, he wrestled more than anyone in the entire village. Balwan Singh enrolled him in the local wrestling school. Bajrang was so fond of wrestling that he often bunked school to go to attend wrestling bouts. Soon he became one of the best wrestlers in the area.

Balwan Singh wanted his son to complete his education, but Bajrang wasn't interested. He told his father that all he wanted to do was wrestle. Knowing his son's capabilities, Balwan Singh didn't pressurize his son to study.

In 2008, when Bajrang was 14, he was spotted by Rampal Singh, who was the coach of Olympian Sushil Kumar. Rampal advised him to join the Chhatrasal Stadium, which is considered one of the best wrestling centres in the country. Bajrang took Rampal's advice and went through a rigorous training programme. There he met Yogeshwar Dutt, who had won a gold medal in the 2003 Commonwealth Games and a bronze in the 2012 Olympic Games.

Yogeshwar Dutt took Bajrang under his wing. Dutt gave tips, fought bouts with his protégé and taught him tricks to trounce the opponent. The teenager toiled to become better at his performance.

> As a child, Bajrang was so fond of wrestling that he would often bunk school to attend wrestling bouts. Soon he became one of the best wrestlers in the area.

Dutt, who was at the peak of his career, advised him to aim higher and never look back.

The Journey

Dutt's mentoring and Bajrang's hard work soon brought results. In 2011, Bajrang won the silver medal at the Cadet World Championships, an annual event held for wrestlers aged between the ages of 16 and 17 years and organized by United World Wrestling (UWW).

The year 2012 saw Bajrang winning many medals in various competitions as he trounced established wrestlers in the junior category. In April 2013, he won the bronze medal at the Asian Wrestling Championships held in New Delhi. He followed it up with another bronze at the World Wrestling Championships in Budapest the same year. This was a turning point in his career.

> Balwan Singh shifted with his family to Sonepat so that Bajrang could attend camps and train at the local SAI centre to better his technique.

Though money was a constraint in the Punia family, his father did his best to provide young Bajrang with every opportunity. When he won his first international medal at the 2013 Asian Wrestling Championships held in Delhi, Balwan Singh realized that his son required family support. In 2015, Balwan left his village and shifted with his family to Sonepat, so that Bajrang could attend camps and train at the local SAI centre. Training at SAI honed his skill and helped him better his technique.

The stamina and power that Bajrang developed at a young age gave him an edge over his rivals. He became a strong contender for international medals alongside his mentor Yogeshwar Dutt. While Bajrang took part in the 61 kg category, Yogeshwar took part in the 65 kg category. In the 2014 Commonwealth Games at Glasgow, Scotland, Yogeshwar won a gold while Bajrang got a silver medal. India had great expectations from the duo and they did not let the country down.

In the 2015 World Wrestling Championships, Bajrang finished in the fifth position. He was new to the global competition scene and had a lot to learn. In 2016, he earned his first international gold medal at the Commonwealth Wrestling Championships held in Singapore.

A wrestling bout comprises two games of three minutes each with a break in between. But those few minutes of wrestling consume a lot of energy and leave the wrestler completely exhausted. So stamina is as essential as strength. It is here that Bajrang scored over most of his opponents. But strength and stamina were not his only assets. His major asset was his technique, which allowed him to assess the strength and weaknesses of his opponent, later striking like lightning.

In the year 2017, Bajrang won a gold medal at the Asian Wrestling Championships in New Delhi in May and a silver medal at the Under 23 World Championships in Poland in November. In 2018 he moved to the higher weight group and won four medals in the 65 kg category. With this win, he gained the position of World Number 1 in that category. He won the silver medal at the 2018 World Wrestling Championships in the 65 kg category.

In November 2018, Yogeshwar Dutt retired from wrestling. He had mentored Bajrang, given him tips and treated him like a younger brother. In his touching farewell speech, he said that if it was not for Bajrang, he would not have quit the mat yet. He had high hopes for Bajrang, who had moved into Dutt's category of 65 kg. The next target was a medal in the Olympics. Yogeshwar had already won a bronze in 2012. It was now up to Bajrang to take it a notch higher and win the gold.

In 2019, Bajrang won a gold medal in the Asian Wrestling Championships and a bronze in the World Championships, qualifying for the 2020 Tokyo Olympics. His dream was about to come true. However, just a month before the Tokyo Olympics, Bajrang suffered a knee injury at the Aliyev Wrestling Competition in Russia, where he was preparing for the Olympics. It was serious and a cause for worry for his coach.

> Braving a serious knee injury, Bajrang strapped a brace around it and competed in the 2020 Tokyo Oylmpics and won a bronze medal.

Bajrang refused to heed the doctor's advice to return to India to get his injury treated. Abandoning the competition was out of the question. It was his first stint at the Olympics and he would risk anything to continue with the bouts. It was a matter of honour for him.

Strapping a brace around his knee, Bajrang went into the ring to face his opponents. On the last day of the competition, ignoring the risks, he took the brace off his knee as it restricted his movement. Bajrang's bronze medal that day was a triumph of willpower. He had suffered agonizing pain and risked a lot so he could win the medal and he had succeeded. Not only did he win a medal, but he also led the Indian contingent in the closing ceremony. Olympian Shako Bentinidis, who was Bajrang's coach, was all praise for his resolve and tenacity.

In the 2022 World Wrestling Championships in Belgrade, Bajrang sustained a head injury during his earlier bout in the pre-quarterfinals. He entered the ring with a bandaged head and was trailing by a point till the last 20 seconds. He was down 6-0 initially, but then he took a magnificent two-pointer in the dying moments. His bout in the Belgrade World Championships despite a head injury was nothing short of heroic.

The bronze was his fourth medal in the World Championships. No Indian wrestler has achieved this feat. He won a silver in 2018 and three bronze medals in 2013, 2019 and 2022.

Bajrang's hard work has won him many awards and recognitions. He was awarded the Arjuna Award in 2015 and in 2019, he received the Rajiv Gandhi Khel Ratna and the Padma Shri. FICCI awarded him the India Sports Award for winning the bronze medal at the Tokyo Olympics.

Bajrang is married to Sangeeta Phogat, who is a silver medallist in the National Wrestling Championships. He works with the Indian Railways as a gazetted officer (sports).

Bajrang's success has motivated many youngsters to take up wrestling and dream of achieving similar success. His advice to them is if you worry about losing, then you can forget about winning. Bajrang now aims to win a gold medal in the 2024 Paris Olympics.

1st Indian Woman Wrestler to win an Olympic Medal

Sakshi Malik

Wrestling

Sakshi Malik: The Freestyle Wrestling Star

The Story

Sakshi Malik was born on 3 September 1992 in a small village called Mokhra in Rohtak, Haryana. Her father, Sukhbir Malik, is a bus conductor and her mother, Sudesh Malik, works in the local Anganwadi. Like many men in Haryana, Sakshi's grandfather, Badhlu Ram, was a wrestler. The wish to become a wrestler was born at an early age when she saw her grandfather wrestle. The little girl listened to her grandfather's stories about *dangals* and bouts with great interest.

Mokhra was a conservative place that did not encourage girls to take up sports, least of all wrestling. Like the Phogat sisters, Sakshi had to fight against all odds to follow her dream. Although the villagers disapproved of the idea, her grandfather encouraged the girl to train to become a wrestler.

Deciding to become a wrestler was easy, but finding a coach for the training was not. A coach who trained a girl for wrestling would face a lot of opposition, so no one wanted to train Sakshi. Finally, it was her passion for the sport that made Ishwar Dahiya agree to train the 12-year-old girl.

But the hurdles were not over for Sakshi. Her coach struggled to find an *akhara* where he could train the girl. The Chhotu Ram Stadium in Rohtak, which had an *akhara* for wrestling, did not allow girls. Ishwar Dahiya had to convince the authorities that Sakshi had the potential to become a good wrestler. Finally, they agreed and Sakshi began training.

The Journey

Ishwar Dahiya faced protests from locals when he took Sakshi under his wing, but he did not give up. Sakshi was subjected to a lot of taunts as she made her way to practice every day. The insults faced by Dahiya and Sakshi strengthened their resolve to prove everyone wrong.

> Sakshi's dream to fly in an airplane came true when she took part in the 2010 Junior World Championships in Budapest.

Sakshi proved to be a hard-working pupil. She followed all instructions and practised sincerely. By her own admission, the desire to travel by air inspired her to work hard. It is important for a wrestler to practice with another of equal strength and weight. Since none of the girls in the village took up wrestling, Sakshi wrestled with boys though she was often taunted and criticized.

Sakshi's dream to fly in an airplane came true when she took part in the 2010 Junior World Championships in Budapest. The championship was her first big break as a professional freestyle wrestler. Sakshi won a bronze medal in the 58 kg category, proving her critics wrong.

That was just the beginning of her success story. She won the bronze medal at the 2013 Commonwealth Championships held in Johannesburg. Thereafter, she took part in the 2014 Dave Schultz International Wrestling Tournament. It is the top annual international wrestling tournament in the USA. Its highlight is the women's freestyle competition, which offers one of the most talent-packed fields of female wrestlers outside of the World Championships. Sakshi went on to win her first gold medal in the tournament and proved that her talent was not a flash in the pan.

The silver medal she won in the 2014 Commonwealth Games in Glasgow remains her favourite. At the 2015 Asian Championships she displayed some aggressive wrestling and clinched a bronze.

Sakshi followed a rigorous diet plan. Although she loves *aloo parathas* and *kadhi-chawal*, she couldn't afford the luxury of having them. She also did vigorous exercises, including 500 sit-ups every day.

Sakshi won many medals at various events, mainly the Asian Championships, but the crowning glory was her bronze medal in the 2016 Rio Olympics. The crucial aspect was that her win finally ended India's long wait for an Olympics medal in the women's freestyle 58 kg category. The whole country celebrated her victory, including the very villagers of Mokhra who had taunted the Malik family for supporting their daughter's dream.

> Sakshi's bronze medal in the 2016 Rio Olympics finally ended India's long wait for an Olympic medal in the women's freestyle 58 kg category.

Despite tasting victory, athletes too have their share of highs and lows. Sakshi went through a depressing time after the 2017 Commonwealth Championships. She had not been able to win any medals, and that sapped her confidence and morale. Instead of giving in to the depression, she worked with a psychologist, who recommended that she begin writing her thoughts regularly in a diary. The results were slow to manifest, but the sessions with the psychologist yielded results.

Sakshi won a bronze medal at the 2018 Commonwealth Games. But much to her disappointment she lost the opportunity to compete in the 2020 Tokyo Olympics. She had moved up to the 62 kg weight category. The Olympics berth went to Sonam Malik, to whom Sakshi had lost four times.

During tough times whenever she considered quitting wrestling, her family and coach rallied around her. They cheered and goaded her on. Qualifying for the 2022 Commonwealth Games worked more than anything in boosting up her confidence. Sakshi felt a burst of energy and optimism at the thought of winning a medal in the 62 kg category. It was the third time she would take part in the Commonwealth Games, having won a silver and a bronze previously.

At the 2022 Commonwealth Games, it was her determination and hard work that helped her clinch the gold medal. Her dream had finally come true. The national anthem played for her win—something she had always wanted. This was her biggest medal after the bronze win at the 2016 Rio Olympics.

With her achievements, Sakshi joined the ranks of the Phogat sisters, who had created history in wrestling. She has placed Rohtak on the world wrestling map. The Chhotu Ram Stadium, where girls were not welcome, is now proud of the women wrestlers.

In 2016, Sakshi was honoured with the Rajiv Gandhi Khel Ratna Award. She received the Padma Shri in 2017. She now works for the Indian Railways.

Sakshi dreams of opening an academy to train Olympic-level wrestlers, which will allow them an opportunity to compete in the future.

Geeta, Babita, Vinesh Phogat: The Terrific Trio

The Story

Mahavir Singh Phogat of Balali in Haryana, known for its wrestling culture, always dreamed of making wrestlers out of his children. It is believed that he wanted to have sons, who would take the wrestling legacy forward. But fate had other plans. On 15 December 1988, Mahavir and Daya Kaur became parents to a daughter. They named her Geeta. The very next year another daughter was born to them, who was named Babita.

Two more daughters, Ritu and Sangeeta, were born in 1994 and 1998 respectively. Tragedy fell on the Phogats when Mahavir's younger brother Rajpal Phogat was killed in a land dispute. Rajpal had two daughters, whom Mahavir took under his wing. Thus, Mahavir now had six girls to look after.

In 2000, when Karnam Malleswari created history by winning a bronze medal in weightlifting at the Sydney Olympics, becoming the first Indian woman to do so, Mahavir watched the event with great excitement. If Malleswari could win a medal at the Olympics, so can my daughters, he thought.

The Phogats had been a family of wrestlers, including Mahavir's father. Since Mahavir didn't have a son then, he decided his daughters would become wrestlers. He shocked his relatives by telling them that he was going to train his daughters. Nothing they said could change his mind.

The Journey

Once he had decided to train the girls, Mahavir did the unthinkable. He made his daughters cut their hair and wear shorts like a sportsperson. He brushed aside his wife's objection and would drag the girls out of their beds at an unearthly hour. Then, he would make them go for long runs in the fields and do several rounds of push-ups and sit-ups. The villagers jeered and ridiculed the girls and their parents.

After a warm-up, the girls would grapple in the mud pit created by Mahavir and then go to school. At school, both teachers and students would express reservations about the girls training to be wrestlers, taunting them often. It was a harrowing time for them. Exhausted after the morning run and bouts of wrestling, the girls would often fall asleep in class. But Mahavir did not change his mind. He continued to put them through a difficult training regimen.

Daya Kaur was worried about her daughters' wedding, but Mahavir had no such worries. He wanted them to win medals on

> Inspired by Karnam Malleswari's Olympic victory, Mahavir decided to train his daughters to become wrestlers. He even brushed aside his wife's objection.

the international stage. Since the village had so far only known male wrestlers, Mahavir decided to make his daughters wrestle with the boys of the village.

Mahavir's strictness paid off when both Geeta and Babita won their first international medals at the 2009 Commonwealth Championships. While Geeta won the medal in the 55 kg category, Babita won it in the 51 kg category. It was a proud moment, not just for Mahavir Singh, but for the entire Balali village. Soon, the villagers too accepted the girls' mettle and gathered at the Phogat family house to congratulate them on their success.

That was just the beginning of the Phogat sisters' success story. The girls repeated their success in 2010 when Geeta created history by becoming the first female Indian wrestler to win gold at the Commonwealth Games, while Babita won a silver. Vinesh Phogat, Mahavir's niece, brought home a bronze from the 2013 Asian Championships. She followed it up with a gold at the 2014 Commonwealth Games and a bronze at the Asian Games later that year.

> Geeta created history in 2010 by becoming the first female Indian wrestler to win gold at the Commonwealth Games.

The Phogat sisters continued to win medals in many national and international events. They returned home with many honours and won the love of the entire country. But Mahavir Singh was not satisfied. He wanted them to win a medal in the Olympic Games.

On a rainy evening in August 2016, Mahavir Singh Phogat watched the Rio Olympics with his family on the television. An air of tension hung over the Phogat house, as Vinesh Phogat was competing in the wrestling event. Mahavir's daughters, Geeta and Babita, had not made the cut for the Olympics, but the niece he had trained was representing India at the event. He was hopeful Vinesh would win a medal.

To Mahavir's disappointment, Vinesh suffered injuries and had to leave the game. But the setback didn't stop her. After surgery and rehabilitation, Vinesh continued winning medals. She won two silver medals at the 2017 and 2018 Asian Championships, a gold medal in the Commonwealth Games, and another one in the Asian Games. In 2019, she won a bronze at the World Championships.

Once again, Vinesh made it to the 2020 Tokyo Olympics, but did not make it past the quarterfinals of the 53 kg category. It was heartbreaking for the Phogat family. It was the second debacle after she lost in the quarterfinals at the 2016 Rio Olympics because of a knee dislocation. Wins and losses are a part of an athlete's life, and Vinesh took it in her stride. The hardworking girl won gold at the 2021 Asian Championships.

Today, Vinesh Phogat is one of the top women wrestlers in the country and the first one to win multiple medals at the World Wrestling Championships. In September 2022, she won the bronze medal in the World Wrestling Championships in Belgrade. This was Vinesh's second bronze medal after she won the first one at the 2019 World Wrestling Championships in Kazakhstan. It came soon after she became a triple champion in the 2022 Commonwealth Games in Birmingham. Vinesh has already set her goal at the 2024 Paris Olympics.

Although the Olympics medal continues to dodge the Phogat sisters, the tally of medals won by them has grown. In addition, Geeta was awarded the Arjuna Award in 2012. Vinesh was honoured with the Arjuna Award in 2016 and the Rajiv Gandhi Khel Ratna Award in 2020.

Mahavir Singh's third daughter, Ritu, won the gold medal at the 2016 Commonwealth Wrestling Championships in the 48 kg category. She is training in Mixed Martial Arts (MMA). Priyanka Phogat, Mahavir's niece, won the silver medal in the 2016 Asian Wrestling Championships.

Geeta was last seen competing in 2019 and now works as Deputy Superintendent of Police in Haryana. Babita joined the Bharatiya Janata Party, while Vinesh continues to aspire for yet another medal. Mahavir lives in the hope of an Olympic medal in the family kitty. With so many wrestlers in the family, it should not be difficult to win one.

The story of the Phogat sisters inspired Aamir Khan to produce a film based on their lives titled *Dangal*.

To read more about their journey,
scan the code below.

Acknowledgements

Authors write manuscripts, not books. The journey of an author's manuscript from words on a page to a book in the hands of readers is a collaborative effort that demands intense dedication and hard work from a team of individuals. The entire process requires active participation from the author, the editors, the cover designer, the typesetter, the illustrator and the proofreader.

This book is the result of countless hours of hard work and determination. The scrupulous research and meticulous sifting through heaps of information has been an overwhelming endeavour, made possible by the invaluable support of many individuals. Thanks to them, this germ of an idea blossomed into a beautiful book. I owe a tremendous debt of gratitude to my family and friends for their support, ideas, knowledge and resources.

I am deeply grateful to Tina Narang for her belief in the book's potential. Immense gratitude to Garima Syal, my editor, for her guidance and untiring effort in moulding the manuscript into a remarkable book. My thanks to Ankita Deshpande and Mini Narayanan for their editorial inputs. I am thankful to Pallavi Jain for the excellent cover design and the beautiful illustrations that breathed life into the book. I thank Kamal Kishor for his inputs on the cover, and the lovely typeset of the book. Finally, a big round of thanks to the entire marketing team at HarperCollins India for taking the book to its readers.

A heartfelt thank you goes to Colonel Devraj Gill, the Commandant, and the staff of the Army Sports Institute (ASI) for their informative and supportive role.

As always, I am grateful to Ajoy, who motivated me to write this book. There were multiple occasions when I felt like giving up, but his unwavering support kept pushing me forward. In his versatile role as a sounding board, beta reader and critic, he effortlessly offers constructive insights. Thank you for being the rock you have always been. None of it would have been possible without your support.

Finally, I owe every bit of my achievement to the readers, whose unwavering support has been the cornerstone of my journey. Thank you for your faith in me.

About the Author

Tanushree Podder is a well-known travel writer and novelist who enjoys writing in various genres. This has led to her writing in historical, military, crime and paranormal genres for adults and children.

Born in New Delhi, she worked in the corporate sector for eight long years before she quit the rat race to write.

Some of her works include *Nurjahan's Daughter*, *Spooky Stories*, *More Spooky Stories*, *Boots Belts Berets*, *A Closetful of Skeletons*, *The Teenage Diary of Rani Laxmibai* and *The Girls in Green* among others. *The Golden Sportspersons* is her nineteenth book.

Three of her books, *Boots Belts Berets*, *A Closetful of Skeletons* and *The Girls in Green* are being adapted into web series.

About the Illustrator

Meet Pallavi, an acclaimed illustrator celebrated for her skilful blend of warmth and intricate detail in her artwork. With a background in Finance and Design, her Mumbai roots enrich her ability to capture the essence of diverse cultures and experiences. From vibrant cityscapes to awe-inspiring landscapes and heartwarming characters, Pallavi's illustrations transport readers on whimsical journeys filled with captivating stories. Honoured with accolades like the Neev Book Award and the Jarul Book Award, Pallavi invites readers to immerse themselves in the magical worlds she brings to life.

In this book, Pallavi breathes life into the stories of Indian sportspersons through captivating portrait illustrations, offering a journey of discovery and inspiration.

Other Timeless Biographies by HarperCollins

An artist, a citizen of the world and a rebel, Amrita Sher-Gil was one of modern India's first professional women artists. Determined to forge a path of her own in the world of art, she went on to become a painter of world renown.

Amrita was born in Hungary, raised in India and trained in France—and she was inspired by writers, musicians and artists across geographies and time. From ancient Indian murals and miniature paintings, to medieval and modern European art, Amrita found lessons everywhere. Take a peek behind the canvas to get to know Amrita the artist, the rebel, the dreamer.

Meet Wing Commander Dr Vijayalakshmi Ramanan, the first female officer in the Indian Air Force; Major Priya Jhingan, the first lady cadet in the Indian Army; and the all-woman Navy crew who circumnavigated the world!

Follow the journeys of these exceptional, path-breaking women in the Indian Armed Forces, who shattered stereotypes and created new opportunities. Interspersed with vivid illustrations, diary entries and blog posts, these stories are sure to inspire young readers.

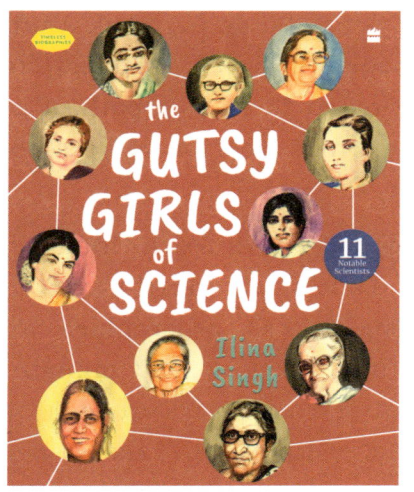

This book explores the contribution of these remarkable Indian women—from cytogeneticist Archana Sharma and botanist Janaki Ammal to mathematician Raman Parimala, physicist Bibha Chowdhuri, chemist Asima Chatterjee and several others.

It is a celebration of their lives and the wonderful world of science.

These 11 exemplary women were recognized by the Indian government in 2020.

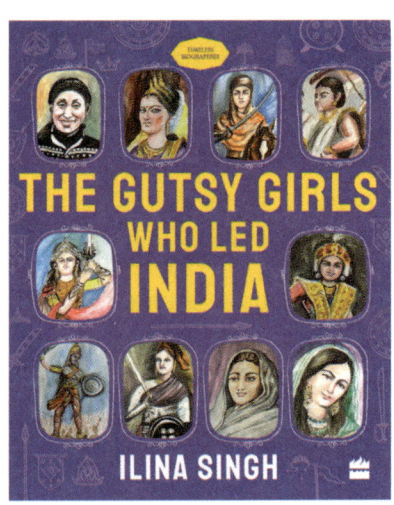

Queen Didda of Kashmir, one of the longest reigning Indian monarchs with forty years on the throne; Velu Nachiyar, the first Indian woman to have led her army to victory against the East India Company; Abakka Chowta, who along with her soldiers attacked ships with flaming arrows and burnt down a few; Keladi Chennamma, who provided shelter to Shivaji's son against the Mughals; Rani Lakshmibai, whose name is synonymous with bravery, sacrifice and leadership, among many other brave and courageous women warriors.

The book also includes portraits of the brave warriors along with activities for children and young adults to explore and develop their own leadership potential.

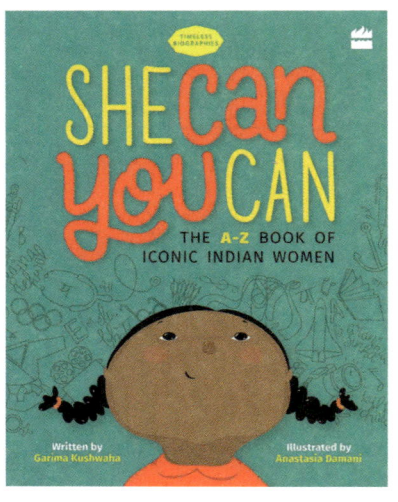

An A to Z biography of iconic Indian women, one for each letter of the English alphabet. Each character is represented by an illustrative sketch and a 500-word summary. This inspirational and motivational book includes the achievements of pioneering female scientists, doctors, activists, painters, dancers, astronauts, comedians, political leaders and many more from different walks of life.

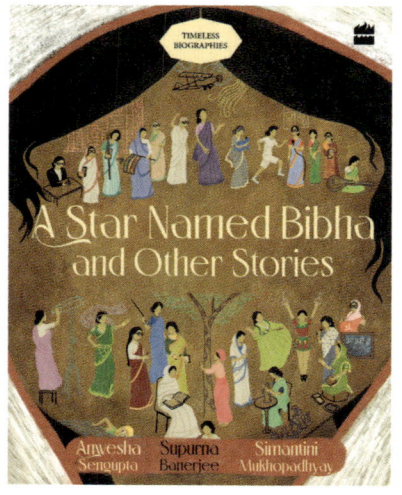

What's a common thread that connects remarkable women such as Tun Tun, Bibha Chowdhury and Pandita Ramabai?

That they were born, lived and worked between the late-nineteenth and mid-twentieth centuries, when being a woman was a challenging experience, shaped by caste, religion, place of residence, class and occupation. These women dared to go against social conventions and made their mark in traditionally male-dominated spaces and professions, paving the way for the women of today.

A Star Named Bibha and Other Stories is a collection of short biographies of thirty such trailblazing Indian women who have broken the glass ceiling, and done it in style. Read about Durgabai Kamat, Amrit Kaur, Amrita Pritam, Fatima Beevi and many other such inspiring women of India.